ASSESSMENT TOOLS

SAGE HUMAN SERVICES GUIDES, VOLUME 30

SAGE HUMAN SERVICES GUIDES

A series of books edited by ARMAND LAUFFER and CHARLES D. GARVIN. Published in cooperation with the University of Michigan School of Social Work and other organizations.

1: **GRANTSMANSHIP** by Armand Lauffer (second edition)
4: **SHARED DECISION MAKING** by Frank F. Maple
5: **VOLUNTEERS** by Armand Lauffer and Sarah Gorodezky with Jay Callahan and Carla Overberger
10: **GROUP PARTICIPATION** by Harvey J. Bertcher
11: **BE ASSERTIVE** by Sandra Stone Sundel and Martin Sundel
14: **NEEDS ASSESSMENT** by Keith A. Neuber with William T. Atkins, James A. Jacobson, and Nicholas A. Reuterman
15: **DEVELOPING CASEWORK SKILLS** by James A. Pippin
17: **EFFECTIVE MEETINGS** by John E. Tropman
19: **USING MICROCOMPUTERS IN SOCIAL AGENCIES** by James B. Taylor
20: **CHANGING ORGANIZATIONS AND COMMUNITY PROGRAMS** by Jack Rothman, John L. Erlich, and Joseph G. Teresa
24: **CHANGING THE SYSTEM** by Milan J. Dluhy
25: **HELPING WOMEN COPE WITH GRIEF** by Phyllis R. Silverman
27: **ORGANIZING FOR COMMUNITY ACTION** by Steve Burghardt
28: **AGENCIES WORKING TOGETHER** by Robert J. Rossi, Kevin J. Gilmartin, and Charles W. Dayton
29: **EVALUATING YOUR AGENCY'S PROGRAMS** by Michael J. Austin, Gary Cox, Naomi Gottlieb, J. David Hawkins, Jean M. Kruzich, and Ronald Rauch
30: **ASSESSMENT TOOLS** by Armand Lauffer
31: **UNDERSTANDING PROGRAM EVALUATION** by Leonard Rutman and George Mowbray
32: **UNDERSTANDING SOCIAL NETWORKS** by Lambert Maguire
33: **FAMILY ASSESSMENT** by Adele M. Holman
35: **SUPERVISION** by Eileen Gambrill and Theodore J. Stein
36: **BUILDING SUPPORT NETWORKS FOR THE ELDERLY** by David E. Biegel, Barbara K. Shore, and Elizabeth Gordon
37: **STRESS MANAGEMENT FOR HUMAN SERVICES** by Richard E. Farmer, Lynn Hunt Monohan, and Reinhold W. Hekeler
38: **FAMILY CAREGIVERS AND DEPENDENT ELDERLY** by Dianne Springer and Timothy H. Brubaker
39: **DESIGNING AND IMPLEMENTING PROCEDURES FOR HEALTH AND HUMAN SERVICES** by Morris Schaefer

40: **GROUP THERAPY WITH ALCOHOLICS** by Baruch Levine and Virginia Gallogly
41: **DYNAMIC INTERVIEWING** by Frank F. Maple
42: **THERAPEUTIC PRINCIPLES IN PRACTICE** by Herbert S. Strean
43: **CAREERS, COLLEAGUES, AND CONFLICTS** by Armand Lauffer
44: **PURCHASE OF SERVICE CONTRACTING** by Peter M. Kettner and Lawrence L. Martin
45: **TREATING ANXIETY DISORDERS** by Bruce A. Thyer
46: **TREATING ALCOHOLISM** by Norman K. Denzin
47: **WORKING UNDER THE SAFETY NET** by Steve Burghardt and Michael Fabricant
48: **MANAGING HUMAN SERVICES PERSONNEL** by Peter J. Pecora and Michael J. Austin
49: **IMPLEMENTING CHANGE IN SERVICE PROGRAMS** by Morris Schaefer
50: **PLANNING FOR RESEARCH** by Raymond M. Berger and Michael A. Patchner
51: **IMPLEMENTING THE RESEARCH PLAN** by Raymond M. Berger and Michael A. Patchner
52: **MANAGING CONFLICT** by Herb Bisno
53: **STRATEGIES FOR HELPING VICTIMS OF ELDER MISTREATMENT** by Risa S. Breckman and Ronald D. Adelman
54: **COMPUTERIZING YOUR AGENCY'S INFORMATION SYSTEM** by Denise E. Bronson, Donald C. Pelz, and Eileen Trzcinski
55: **HOW PERSONAL GROWTH AND TASK GROUPS WORK** by Robert K. Conyne
56: **COMMUNICATION BASICS FOR HUMAN SERVICE PROFESSIONALS** by Elam Nunnally and Caryl Moy
57: **COMMUNICATION DISORDERS IN AGING** edited by Raymond H. Hull and Kathleen M. Griffin
58: **THE PRACTICE OF CASE MANAGEMENT** by David P. Moxley
59: **MEASUREMENT IN DIRECT PRACTICE** by Betty J. Blythe and Tony Tripodi
60: **BUILDING COALITIONS IN THE HUMAN SERVICES** by Milan J. Dluhy with the assistance of Sanford L. Kravitz
61: **PSYCHIATRIC MEDICATIONS** by Kenneth J. Bender
62: **PRACTICE WISDOM** by Donald F. Krill
63: **PROPOSAL WRITING** by Soraya M. Coley and Cynthia A. Scheinberg
64: **QUALITY ASSURANCE FOR LONG-TERM CARE PROVIDERS** by William Ammentorp, Kenneth D. Gossett, and Nancy Euchner Poe

A **SAGE** HUMAN SERVICES GUIDE **30**

ASSESSMENT TOOLS

For Practitioners, Managers, and Trainers

Armand LAUFFER

*Published in cooperation with the University of Michigan
School of Social Work*

SAGE PUBLICATIONS
The International Professional Publishers
Newbury Park   London   New Delhi

To my son Josh,
Whose search into what is
And concern over what will be
Are superseded only by his commitments
To what ought to be.

For information address:

SAGE Publications, Inc.
2455 Teller Road
Newbury Park, California 91320

SAGE Publications Ltd.
6 Bonhill Street
London EC2A 4PU
United Kingdom

SAGE Publications India Pvt. Ltd.
M-32 Market
Greater Kailash I
New Delhi 110 048 India

Printed in the United States of America

Library of Congress Cataloging in Publication Data

Lauffer, Armand.
    Assessment tools.

    (Sage human services guides ; v. 30)
    "Published in cooperation with the University of
Michigan School of Social Work."
    1. Social work administration—Evaluation.   2. Social
service—Planning.   3. Evaluation research (Social
action programs)   I. University of Michigan. School of
Social Work.   II. Title.   III. Series.
HV41.L318   1982   361'.0068   82-10552
ISBN 0-8039-1007-X

FOURTH PRINTING, 1991

CONTENTS

Acknowledgments and a Confession   6

1. Using Assessment Tools   7

2. Where It's At: The Use of Mapping Tools   17

3. Task Analysis: Doin' What You Oughta   43

4. The Nominal Group Technique: Setting an
   Action Agenda   63

5. The Delphi Is No Oracle   91

6. May the Force Be with You: Using
   Force Field Analysis   121

7. Gaming: Making Believe for Real   135

8. Images of Reality: Photography as an
   Assessment Tool   165

9. Putting It All Together: The Contingency
   Approach to Assessment   176

About the Author   192

ACKNOWLEDGMENTS
AND A CONFESSION

I have a confession to make. I didn't write this book. I compiled it. Many of the tools described were developed by other people or were tested by them in practice.

Task analysis, for example, was developed by Sydney Fine when he was in government, and later at the Upjohn Institute. The nominal group technique was developed and tested by Andrew H. Van de Ven and André Delbecq. Much of the discussion on Delphi draws on the work of Murray Turoff and is based on the creation of the instrument by Norman Dalkey and others at the Rand Corporation. Force field analysis has been around for many years. It draws on the work of Kurt Lewin and his hundreds of followers throughout the world.

I am also indebted to the work of a number of former students and colleagues who have experimented with new and different applications of each tool. They include George Mink, Tom Morton, Lynn Nybell, Carla Overberger, Ellen Saalberg, and Celeste Sturdebant-Reed, as well as others whose names are listed in the appropriate chapters. My own modest contribution was to bring these materials together and to design ways in which you can learn them easily and apply them in your own practice. Each chapter, in fact, looks to and draws from practice.

The vignettes that appear at the beginning of each tools chapter are drawn from my own experiences as well as those of fellow human service professionals throughout the United States, Canada, and Israel. Your own use of these tools is bound to expand on those experiences. If you find them useful, why not let us know? I'm always looking for new applications and promise to share them with students and colleagues, or perhaps in later editions of this book.

Armand Lauffer
Ann Arbor, 1982

1. USING ASSESSMENT TOOLS

None of us would consider developing a treatment plan without careful assessment of the client's problem, potential, or aspirations, and of resources in the immediate environment that might be activated on the client's behalf. Yet we often engage in program design and development paying only cursory attention to the assessment process, relying all too heavily on our intuitions, assuming the correctness of our decisions on the basis of personal and professional commitments.

In the following chapters, I will be sharing with you a number of assessment tools that social workers and others have found useful at many levels of intervention. I will be drawing on their experiences in direct practice with individuals and families, in organizing voluntary associations at the community level, in training and staff development activities, in program planning, and in agency management. These are remarkably flexible tools. You should find it easy to adapt them to your practice. They do not require technical sophistication. They do, however, require some practice.

You will have an opportunity to practice alone or with colleagues and clients as you complete each chapter. Case illustrations will be followed by a discussion of the history of each tool and its multiple uses. A number of examples of the tool adapted for different purposes will be included. I suspect you will have no difficulty in using many of these examples in dealing with an assessment issue currently before you. You may wish to modify the tool for a specific application. There will be suggestions on how to do just that. In the final chapter, I will share with you some of my experiences in using several tools in tandem or in sequence in order to assess the multiple dimensions of a problem or situation or in trying to comprehend it better.

Because the methods and technology used in an assessment are often the same as those of an evaluation and because both activities may take place concurrently, both terms are sometimes used interchangeably. The two, however, are conceptually distinct. Assessment focuses on the examination of what *is*, on what is *likely to be,* or on what *ought to be*. Evaluation focuses on what happened, how it happened, and whether it should have happened. This guide will deal only with assessment.

As you work your way through each chapter, you will find that assessment tools do more than give you information. They help you to structure the information-finding process and lead you to making decisions about the kinds of intervention that may be warranted. That in itself is a good reason to use more than one tool. Different tools lead you to ask different questions and therefore to consider different action options. Moreover, you will discover that there are distinct advantages to using different tools with clients and other consumers, co-workers, policymakers, and so on. Many of the tools were designed to be used in interactional contexts. In this lies their greatest strength. By involving others in the assessment process, you will also be sharing with them the responsibility for programming. You will be energizing them and stimulating their further involvement in problem solving. You will also provide them with a structure through which they can make decisions based on the facts they have uncovered.

It is not necessary for you to read the chapters in the order they appear. Look over the vignettes in each and select those in which you are most interested or that you think will be most useful. Come back to the others when you think they will apply to a work-related situation. This is a book you can read in sections, as each is of particular use to you.

Before moving on, it is important that we distinguish three orientations to assessment: here-and-now, anticipatory, and normative assessment. Most of the tools described can be used for each, although you may find some more useful than others in given situations.

ASSESSING WHAT IS, WHAT MIGHT BE,
AND WHAT OUGHT TO BE

When we assess what is, we are directing our attention to the *here-and-now*. We might choose to examine the services currently being provided, the populations being served, or the relationships among providers and between providers and consumers. We might also be looking at the environment that surrounds the provision of services. Wherever one focuses, it is important to know what questions to ask. When the practitioner or program planner focuses on an actual or potential consumer population, the following questions might be asked:

(1) To what extent do *debilitating or inappropriate attitudes, values, and perspectives* limit people's abilities to make use of available resources or to act on their own behalf?
(2) To what extent are they *unaware of available services,* programs, and facilities or the benefits and costs of making use of them?
(3) To what extent do they have the *capacity or skill* to make use of these programs or services?

Answers to those questions may lead some practitioners toward an advocacy or broker strategy aimed at empowerment, *animation* or *conscienization*. It might lead others to view potential consumers as deviants whose attitudes and behaviors must be reshaped. The ideological position of the assessor may have much to do with whether the population being assessed is viewed as victim, deviant, or client. Thus, the same questions asked by different persons are likely to yield a variety of answers.

The answers to these questions are likely to differ further from those of the practitioner or planner who focuses on the programs or services to a particular population rather than the population itself. Here, five questions might be asked:

(1) To what extent are services of various kinds *available,* and to whom?
(2) To what extent are available services *accessible* (by dint of location, hours offered, and removal of architectural and psychological or social barriers)?
(3) Even if available and accessible, are services *responsive* to actual and potential consumers, and what kinds of *accountability* mechanisms are built in to those services?

(4) How *effective* are the services (that is, do they make a difference, and for whom)?

(5) Are they *efficient* (could one serve larger numbers or provide more comprehensive services for the same amount of money, or would a change in the scope of the program result in considerable cost saving)?

When one examines the relationships among service providers or between providers and consumers, at least two sets of questions are raised:

(1) To what extent are services provided *comprehensively,* in such a way that one service complements another instead of competing for the client's allegiance or leaving large service areas uncovered?

(2) Are services provided *continuously,* so that when one agency completes its service (for example, job training in an institutional setting), other agencies are ready to provide subsequent service (re-entry counseling for the disabled person's family, job placement in the local community, and other supports leading to independent living arrangements)?

These are here-and-now types of questions. They focus on *what is.* In *anticipatory* assessment one asks the same kinds of questions, but the focus is on the extent to which these problems are likely to be felt in the future. One might make projections on the bases of anticipated or unanticipated changes. What might be the likely drain on existing services should unemployment double or triple in the next five years? Would one wish, then, to focus on the debilitating attitudes of our clients or on their lack of marketable skills? Or, assuming current trends and the completion of the legislation processes aimed at shifting responsibilities from the public to the private sector, and from federal to state and local jurisdictions, to what extent might one anticipate continued problems of program availability, accessibility, accountability, effectiveness, or efficiency?

The advantages of anticipatory assessment are that it permits practitioners and program planners to think ahead rather than to catch up with problems after the fact. It enables us to make decisions now that are likely to head off problems and their consequences for the populations for which we are mandated to provide services.

There is yet a third approach. *Normative* assessment begins with an image of a desired state. We might ask ourselves what kind of services we would like to see in place four or five years from now, or what kinds of capacities we would like clients, staff members, or target populations to develop. We also might begin by deciding what a minimally acceptable service program might look like (perhaps in terms of such issues as availability, accessibility, accountability, effectiveness, and efficiency). In effect, what we would be doing is developing a "competency" model that describes the desired state of affairs.

When a planning and allocating body (like a United Fund or the Welfare Federation or an area agency on aging) establishes minimum standards for service agencies, for example, it establishes a competency model. Professional associations and accrediting bodies (like the Child Welfare League of America and the American Hospital Association) do the same. For assessment purposes, designing the model is only the first step. We would then examine where the population or the service system is now in relationship to the norms we have specified. It is the gap between current reality and the desired state of affairs that would direct us in our program development efforts. Once we have uncovered present levels of competency and compared them to the norms we desire, we would then specify our objectives and set priorities on the bases of salience (importance) and feasibility.

I have often been asked which approach (here-and-now, anticipatory, or normative) works best. Obviously, there is no single answer. We often do the here-and-now kinds of assessments because we are concerned with problems in the here-and-now. Such problems confront us in the present and demand our attention. Yet agencies involved in ongoing planning and program development activities would hardly do themselves or their consumers justice without also engaging in both normative and anticipatory assessment activities.

FOCUSING ON THE ENVIRONMENT

I have always found it useful to focus on the environment around a client system, a service agency, a program, or an issue

with which I am concerned. Two aspects of the environment are
of particular importance—one that might be termed the "acceptance" environment, and one that is called by sociologists the
role-set or "task" environment. In the chapter on ecomapping, we
will examine tools for exploring the role-set and task environment. At this point, however, I want to explore implications of
the acceptance environment.

Around any program, issue, or proposed solutions to the problems, there will tend to be consensus, indifference, or disagreement. Research on community intervention programs suggests
that it is quite appropriate to use a collaborative strategy when
there is consensus that a problem exists or a proposed solution
will work. The same holds true in a family situation in which
everyone agrees on the problem or need for intervention. In such
cases, the practitioner or planner might play an enabling or facili-
tator role, serving as a guide or catalyst, a convenor, a mediator, a
consultant, or even a coordinator. Those in accord would be
brought together in some structured relationship (family treatment, group therapy, task group, or committee) in order to work
together toward a mutually desired outcome. The presumption
would be one of goodwill, of complementarity of objectives. The
practitioner, staff developer, or planner would perform most
effectively as an orchestrator of that consensus.

But the worker would be required to play a very different role
in an environment characterized by indifference. One would
hardly be able to convene the interested parties if they were dis-
interested. When no one seems to care, or at least to care very
much, the interventionist must engage in a consciousness-raising
or campaign strategy. It is necessary to heighten the sensitivity
and awareness of targeted individuals or populations, animating
those who are most directly affected by the problem. The worker's
aim would be to move toward a consensus environment in which
newly interested parties could be activated to work in collaboration toward a given end or ends.

But what if the environment is one in which there are differences
of opinion, conflicts of interest, and disagreement over problems,
ends, and means? Under these circumstances, campaign efforts

aiming to "sell" or to persuade the other side, or to bring the competing sides together, are not likely to prove successful. To the contrary, attempting to mediate a conflict that represents real differences and in which none of the parties sees any advantages to accommodations may prove counterproductive. It might be more appropriate to increase the coercive or reward power of those parties the interventionist represents or whose interest the program aims to serve. In effect, we are suggesting an advocacy model. Consumers and consumer groups might themselves be empowered to take action on their own behalf. Initially, at least, those who oppose the program would not be viewed as potential collaborators. To the contrary, they would be viewed as the opposition—to be isolated or overcome.

How a caseworker, family therapist, staff developer, or community organizer defines the "acceptance" environment, then, has serious implications for planning strategy. You may have noticed that I have been discussing this form of environmental assessment from a here-and-now perspective. But what if we were to take an anticipatory or a normative approach? In the former, we might ask ourselves to what extent there is likely to be consensus, indifference, or disagreement at some point in the future. We might decide, for example, that disagreement today is likely to be diffused if we do not attack it directly and that moving from a climate of confrontation to an environment of indifference might lead to a greater chance of success. This might suggest a temporary strategy of benign neglect. By diffusing a current conflict, we could move progressively toward a consensus that might lead toward collaborative efforts.

Using the normative approach, one might begin with a model of a desired environment. Decisions about what to do today or tomorrow would then flow from an assessment of the implications of one or more of those actions for the environment. A good example might be found in the effort to create appropriate community placements for former mental hospital patients, for the developmentally disabled, or for those who are wards of the corrections system. What kinds of supportive services might be needed? How might the local community or neighborhood be involved in the process of site location? Most important for purposes of assessing the acceptance environment, how would actions taken increase the likelihood of support or opposition in the future?

Keep some of these questions in mind as you read the chapters that follow and as you gain some experience with the tools described. Although each is designed to focus on a particular problem or on the needs of individuals, groups or organizations, and their capacities, the information you are likely to generate and the intervention strategies that may flow from that information are likely to be significantly influenced by the acceptance environment.

THE TOOLS TO BE MASTERED

By the time you complete each chapter, you should have developed beginning mastery of the use of the tool covered. We will be working on seven tools together. *Mapping techniques* are used to understand the ecological relationships between an individual, work group, organization, or some other social system and elements in its environment. They can be used to examine current or anticipated relationships and to explore the ramifications of moving from where we currently are to where we want to go. Like any map, they describe relationships in space and can be used for guiding us in our movements through that space.

Task analysis is in many ways a variant of pictographic mapping. It uses words in the form of "mapping sentences" to specify actual or desired behavior and to show the functional relationships of the tasks that might be performed in a given "job." The *nominal group technique,* as its name implies, uses a grouplike, if not a pure group, process. It was designed to give individuals with disparate interests, capacities, information, or influence equal access to the decision-making and priority-setting processes.

Delphi questionnaires can be used for similar purposes. They can be designed to explore the likelihood of certain future events or processes when neither consensus nor adequate information exists. They also can be used to provide disparate individuals equal access to a policy exploration or decision-making process.

2. WHERE IT'S AT
The Use of Mapping Tools

ILLUSTRATIONS FROM PRACTICE

Illustration 2.1: Families in Space

If your experience is anything like mine, you may find it difficult to structure the first or second interview in a family treatment process. I know some therapists prefer the session to be unstructured, permitting family members to contribute whatever is on their minds. But I think that is awkward for everyone and generally leads to some unproductive work. I think it is important for the family to be doing something together, and the therapist can help them do it. A most effective beginning technique for determining where family members are in relation to each other, and where the family is in its total space, is the ecomap. It invariably gives the participants a sense of where each of them and the family as a whole stand in their environment.

The technique is rather simple. You begin with a large sheet of paper. I always put it on the round table at which I work with clients. A newsprint pad works well, because it gives everyone a chance to write. I start with a circle in the middle of the page, in which each member writes his or her name. I then ask family members with whom they have outside contacts that they think are significant for the family or its members. "Well, Molly sees her physical therapist and Ralph goes to the orthodontist at least once a week," the husband might say. So we draw in another circle for health care and

*list those providers seen by family members. As the session
goes on, we might add other circles for school, friends,
recreational activities, extended family, church, and so on. By
the time the hour is up, it is amazing how much information
we have brought to the surface.*

*We know who is connected where, and who is relatively
unconnected; we know which family members participate
together or relate with outsiders; and we have generated a lot
of information about how they feel about those contacts. A
technique I use in later sessions is drawing up a similar map
about the kinds of connections and contacts family members
would like to have. It is then possible to examine where
people are "at" and where they would like to be individually
or as a collectivity.*

*If you are going somewhere, you might as well know where
you are going and have some idea of how to get there. It may
sometimes be fun to take a drive without any particular
destination in mind. But that is not why people come to
family therapy. They come to find out where they are, to be
clear about where they want to be, and to draw a map on
how to get there.*

Illustration 2.2: No One Takes This Agency Seriously

*It was obvious that there was something wrong with this
place even before I took the job. Funding was drying up. The
agency was getting hardly any client referrals, and no one was
accepting the agency's out referrals. Staff members were
complaining that no one seemed to know the agency existed.
To tell you the truth, that is in part what attracted me to the
place. I'm a builder, and a challenge is what energizes me.*

*When I took over as director, the first thing I did was to
examine the agency's linkages to the outside world. My worst
suspicions were confirmed. If there was such a thing as
"organizational psychiatry," this place would've been relegated
to a booby hatch. It's not that people were doing anything
wrong. As a matter of fact, they were doing just about
everything right. But nobody else seemed to notice. It was
almost like watching a shortstop out on the playing field*

doing everything that a shortstop is supposed to do, using exquisite form. But imagine, if you will, that nobody else is on the field; the shortstop has no team and there's no opposing team. What would you call that behavior? Psychotic, right? The agency was like that.

They sent out referrals to other organizations that clearly couldn't accept their clients. They sent out beautifully written proposals to funders that had no money for their kinds of programs. And they followed rules and procedures that no one required them to follow.

In one of my first staff meetings, I asked everyone to help me understand where the agency fits in the community, the kind of organizational roles it played and with whom. It gave everybody a chance to contribute. After all, I was new and they were educating me. And it provided me with an opportunity to help them discover something that was clear to me.

By putting the agency in the center of the map and identifying all the other organizations in its environment, we could identify with which they had effective linkages and with which almost no linkages existed. We were also able to identify those linkages (like for funding) that were workable in earlier years but no longer seemed to have any payoffs in today's funding environment. You know, the results were amazing. It's not just that we surfaced a lot of information, but it's how it happened.

Workers who had apparently never contributed to staff meetings before were sharing their knowledge with others for the very first time. And as we talked, it became increasingly clear that as an organization we were poorly connected. And sometimes, as the bookkeeper had pointed out, "without connections you might be awfully good at what you do, but nobody will take you too seriously."

MAPPING THE ENVIRONMENT

The use of ecomapping tools provides you with a visual framework for assessing the balance between an organism and its environment. Think back a moment to the two vignettes you just read.

In the first, a family therapist demonstrates an awareness of the sensitive balance that exists between the family and family members, and their environment. Clearly, each member lives a life apart from the family, interacting within and with social, cultural, educational, and work-related elements in his or her external environment. But the whole family is affected by those interactions. In effect, we are talking about a complex psycho-ecological system in which both family members and the total family are part of the environment and, in a sense, the environment is a part of the family. How family members behave toward each other and how they work as a unit often depend on the kinds of interactions they have with elements in that environment.

To understand the nature of these relationships, it may be helpful to think together for a moment about the shortstop referred to by the new administrator in the second vignette. Being a team member requires having a team to be a member of. The roles we play do not exist in isolation from the roles played by other persons with whom we interact. Sociologists call these other role performers participants in the "role set." Each one of us may have an idea of how to perform a given role—parent, secretary, clinician. But if our perceptions are out of synch with the perceptions of others in our role set (children or spouse, co-workers or bosses, clients and colleagues), we're not likely to be performing our roles as expected. When this happens, we experience a good deal of role strain and perhaps even role conflict.

In effect, what happens in any role we play is that we modify our perceptions and the way in which we "ought" to play that role in response to the expectations and the reinforcements provided by people in our role set. When these perceptions are in conflict, we try to modify other people's perceptions or change our own behaviors so as to reach some kind of accommodation which we call "adaptation." It is under conditions of "maladaptation" that intervention in the environment, or with the individual and family, may be necessary.

The same holds true with larger organisms like social agencies, neighborhoods, communities, or even nation-states. Just as it is possible to map out the relationships between the person and significant others in his or her environment (role/role-set relations), it is possible to examine the relationships between an organization and its "organization set." The sociological literature frequently describes the organization set as made up of all the elements in an organization's "task environment." In order to survive, grow, or accomplish its missions, the organization must establish appropriate relationships with key elements in that task environment. From the agency administrator's perspective, it is essential to establish those kinds of environmental relationships that are likely to generate resources and legitimacy and to provide opportunities for sharing responsibility with other organizations and with client groups whose problems are being addressed.

If, on the other hand, you are a community organizer or a social planner and your concern is with changing the behavior of the organization itself, you might find it strategically sound to effect changes in the way in which elements in the organization's environment interact with that organization. Managing the direction or redirection of the flow of resources to an agency may be the quickest way to get it to change the programs and services it offers a client population. Although the web of relationships between individuals or organizations and their environments are complex and often seem to defy comprehension, one way to "get a handle" on them is to chart the relationships on paper. That is what ecomapping is all about.

In the three exercises that follow, I will introduce you to three ecomapping techniques. The first is useful in working with individuals and families. The second explores the relationship between an agency and elements of its task environment. The third provides you with a way of charting the linkages between an organization and its actual or potential collaborators at the community level. Each can be used as described, with little or no modification. You may find all three useful in your work with clients, as training tools with agency staff, in program planning or problem solving with your colleagues, or in planning larger-scale community interventions.

It is also possible that you will not find these exercises terribly useful at this stage in your professional work because they do not deal with issues of concern to you. You may, for example, be more concerned with networking relationships in the neighborhood or with the range of exchanges that take place between lay and professional care providers. Certainly, those relationships can be mapped out as a way of assessing what is, what ought to be, or what is likely to be in the near future. If you have not used mapping tools before, however, I think you will find it helpful to learn from the three activities that follow. Do them by yourself or with colleagues in order to become familiar with the mapping process. Then use ecomapping for whatever purposes you have in mind.

ACTIVITIES

Activity 2.1: Families in Space—
Assessing the Family Ecology

Prior to using an ecomap with individuals or families in treatment, it is a good idea to become familiar with the mapping process yourself. Practice by designing your own ecomap. Do one with or "on" a co-worker so that you can both get the hang of it and can explore its potentials together. You might begin with a blank sheet of paper, perhaps a piece of newsprint. The very openness leads to creativity. On the other hand, if you are new at ecomapping or if you feel that the clients with whom you work need some structure upon which to focus, it is probably not a bad idea to begin with a semistructured map similar to that devised by Ann Hartman (Figure 2.1).

For this exercise, I have chosen to quote liberally from Hartman, who uses the ecomapping process extensively in work with potentially adoptive parents and in other forms of family guidance and treatment.[1]

1. With the exception of Figure 2.5, the text and figures on pages 23-30 are from her *Finding Families: An Ecological Approach to Family Assessment in Adoption* (© 1979, Sage Publications, Inc.).

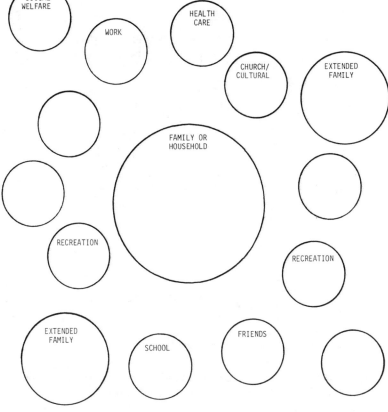

ECO-MAP

Name _____

Date _____

SOCIAL WELFARE

WORK

HEALTH CARE

CHURCH/ CULTURAL

EXTENDED FAMILY

FAMILY OR HOUSEHOLD

RECREATION

RECREATION

EXTENDED FAMILY

SCHOOL

FRIENDS

Fill in connections where they exist.
Indicate nature of connections with a descriptive word or by drawing different kinds of
 lines; ——— for strong, ------- for tenuous, +++++ for stressful.
Draw arrows along lines to signify flow of energy, resources etc. ➔ ➔ ➔
Identify significant people and fill in empty circles as needed.

Figure 2.1

Within the large circle in the middle of the ecomap, chart the members of the household. This is done as follows: A woman is indicated by a circle: ○ ; a man, by a square □. A married couple is portrayed as follows:

It is often useful to add their names and ages. Perhaps, Bill and Ann have two sons, also living in the home.

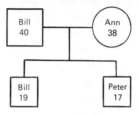

Ann's mother came to live with them after her father died.

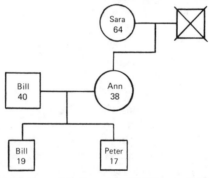

This, then, is a picture of the household. The usefulness of pictures is already demonstrated when one considers the number of words it would take to communicate the facts represented in the ecomap.

A single parent, divorced, mother of one son, and living with her parents, would be pictured as follows:

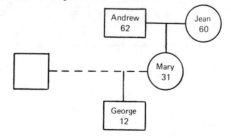

Having pictured the household within the large circle in the middle of the ecomap, the next step is to begin to draw in the connections between the family and the different parts of the ecological environment. Some of the most common systems in the lives of most families, such as work, extended family, recreation, health care, school, and so on, have been labeled in the blank map. Other circles have been left undesignated so that the map is sufficiently flexible to be individualized for different families.

Connections between the family and the various systems are indicated by drawing lines between the family and those systems. The nature of the connection may be expressed by the type of line drawn. A solid or thick line indicates an important or strong connection. A broken line indicates a tenuous connection. A hatched line shows a stressful or conflicted relationship. It is also very useful to indicate the direction of the flow of resources, energy, or interest by drawing arrows along the connecting lines.

In testing out the ecomap, we have found that the use of the three kinds of lines for conflicted, strong, and tenuous relationships is an efficient shorthand when the worker uses the ecomapping procedure as an analytic tool without the family's direct participation. When using the map as an interviewing tool, however, this type of line code has often been felt to be too constraining. Workers prefer to ask applicants to describe the nature of the connection and then qualify that connection by writing a descriptive word or two along the connecting line.

Some of the connections may be drawn to the family or household as a whole when they are intended to portray the total group's relationship with some system in the environment. Other connections may be drawn between a particular individual and an outside system when that person is the only one involved or when different family members are involved with an outside system in different ways. This differentiation enables the map to highlight contrasts in the way various family members are connected with the world.

It is easy to learn to do the ecomap, and it is important to become comfortable with it before using it with adoptive applicants. A simple way to learn is to do one's own ecomap. It is also useful to practice with a friend or two.

The primary use of the ecomap is as an interviewing and assessment tool, to be used as a springboard for discussion and as a visual aid around which to integrate the details of the adoptive family's relationship with the ecological environment. The ecomapping session is a good time to include not only any children in the family, but also other important people in the life space—for example, a grandparent who lives in the home or nearby.

The process of mapping invites active participation. After all, it is the family's map, and no one knows their world as they do. The task of mapping is shared, and the participatory relationship is expressed in action as worker and family tend to move closer together and end shoulder-to-shoulder, absorbed in the joint project.

The kinds of material and relationships that may emerge from work on the mapping process are varied and may range from a rather simple and straightforward assessment of the resources available to a complex analysis of the different ways different family members are relating to the world.

The Tom and Pam Smith ecomap (Figure 2.2) pictures a family with many resources and interests. They have rewarding social connections with friends and community, and have relationships of mutual aid with extended family members. There is stress, of course, as there is in any family. For example, Tom and Pam are concerned about Tom's recently widowed and aging father, and Tom's job, although paying well, makes extremely heavy demands on his time and energy.

The marital pair enjoy some activities together but also have separate interests. In terms of the two children in the family, Paula left the parental home for an early marriage, and the adoptive applicants are very young grandparents. There appears to be some stress around Peter's school life, although he has many friends and is active in sports.

Two quite different maps of two single parent families of similar structure follow. In the map of George's world (Figure 2.3), it is apparent that he and his son are isolated socially and have few sources of support and stimulation. In fact, George, his son, and his mother, who participated together in the mapping session, give evidence of being a rather closed system. Is George's interest in adopting a six- to nine-year-old boy an effort to deal with the family's loneliness and his wish to "give" his son a sibling to heal his aloneness? What potential burden would this imply for a child coming into this home?

William Downs' map (Figure 2.4) portrays a family of similar demographic characteristics, including occupation, income, and

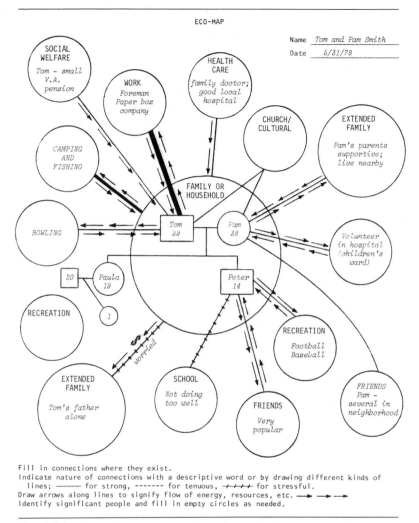

ECO-MAP

Name *Tom and Pam Smith*

Date *5/31/78*

Fill in connections where they exist.
Indicate nature of connections with a descriptive word or by drawing different kinds of
    lines; ——— for strong, ------- for tenuous, ⫫⫫⫫⫫ for stressful.
Draw arrows along lines to signify flow of energy, resources, etc. ——➤ ——➤ ——➤
Identify significant people and fill in empty circles as needed.

Figure 2.2

structure. However, in this map we see an open system with a
variety of lively connections with the life space. An examination of
the ecological system gives evidence of many sources of support
and stimulation, opportunities for self-actualization and development. The system looks rich enough in human resources to meet
the needs of another young person coming into the situation.

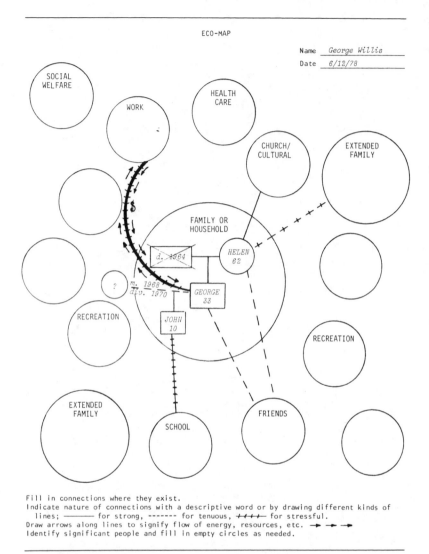

ECO-MAP

Name *George Willis*
Date *6/12/78*

Fill in connections where they exist.
Indicate nature of connections with a descriptive word or by drawing different kinds of
   lines; ————— for strong, ------- for tenuous, ++++ for stressful.
Draw arrows along lines to signify flow of energy, resources, etc. → → →
Identify significant people and fill in empty circles as needed.

Figure 2.3

In the map shown in Figure 2.5, George, Helen, John, and the
worker study it together, the visual image of isolation and social
impoverishment may be shared. The worker may comment, "This
looks like a very lonely family to me." Such an observation may
lead to further exploration of the family's pattern of excluding
contact and drawing away from the world. Out of this kind of

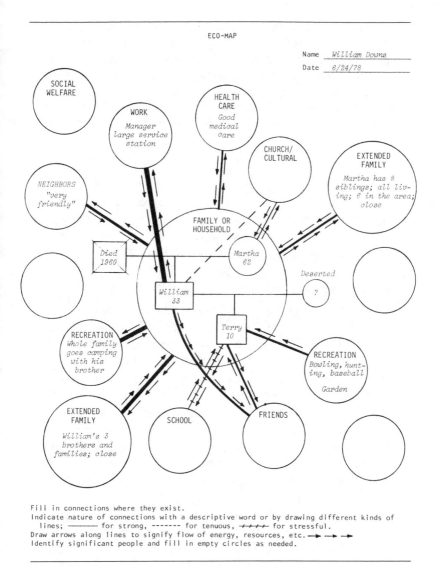

Figure 2.4

discussion may come a recognition on the family's part of some of this loneliness, and of the wish to adopt as a solution to the family's difficulties in developing and maintaining social connections.

Not only does the ecomap lead to an assessment of the family's life situation but, in this case, it could also lead to a decision and a plan. A child cannot heal a family's pain. The task that lies ahead for George and his family is to prepare for adoption by opening up the boundaries of their isolated family and building connections with the world. This very process may diminish the wish for a child and the request may be withdrawn. On the other hand, should George's interest in adoption persist, the worker and George may continue to work together toward the achievement of the goal.

*   *   *

Although Hartman's examples are all drawn from adoptions practice, you will undoubtedly have perceived the utility of eco-mapping with families in other forms of interpersonal helping. With whom will you use it? What difficulties do you perceive in implementing the process? What do you think it may lead to?

Activity 2.2: Mapping the Task Environment

If you are an agency administrator like the newly appointed director quoted in the second vignette, you are undoubtedly aware of how integrally related your organization's operations are with various elements in its environment. Planners and community organizers know that the most direct way to induce change is sometimes the most indirect way: by impacting on the elements in an organization's task environment, thus changing the rules under which it operates, or redirecting the flow of resources into or out of the organization's orbit. Staff developers know that other agency employees are too often ignorant of the task environment and its impact on the organization to perform their jobs appropriately.

The task environment, as its name implies, is made up of all those elements in the general environment that directly impact on the agency's ability to perform its tasks—achieve its objectives. Put another way, it is composed of these organizations and institutions, groups and populations without which a service program could not exist and without which it would have no function to play. These elements include:

(1) those organizations and institutions that provide *auspice and legitimacy* to the program or organization;

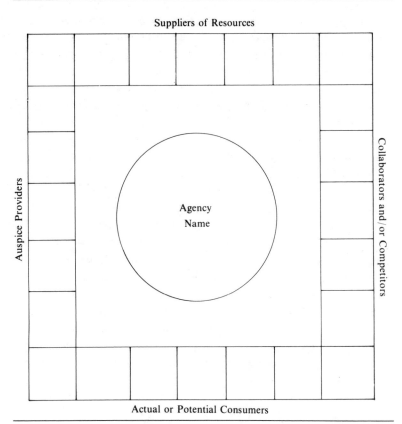

Figure 2.5   Task-Environment Map

(2) providers of *necessary resources;*

(3) the *consumers* of service;

(4) the *competitors* for both resources and consumers; and

(5) the various *collaborators* that enhance the availability, assessibility, accountability, effectiveness, and efficiency, of programs and services.

A word about each. The nature of the program or the service to be developed is very much a creature of the organization or the legislation that provides its auspice and gives it its legitimacy. By *auspice* I mean the organizational and legislative configuration that mandates the program or service and is responsible for seeing that it is implemented. The auspice may be an act that creates a program or service and the rules that govern it, a board of directors, or a federated structure like a United Way organization.

Most service programs utilize a wide variety of tangible *resources:* money, facilities, equipment, and supplies. They also use intangibles like expertise, organizational and personal energy, political influence, and prestige. Intangibles are no less important than tangible resources. The availability of money and facilities, for example, while important, might yield little without the energy and commitment required to activate them. We are all familiar with excellent service programs that were developed without any external sources of financial support.

The more dependent a service organization is on a single source supply, the less likely that it will be able to respond with flexibility to new challenges and demands. The same is true if it becomes dependent on only one or two types of resources. An organization that can shift its programs to accommodate ups and downs in financial support by increasing or decreasing volunteer and consumer inputs, for example, is likely to accommodate to a new challenge and respond to new opportunities. The program developer, therefore must be able to assess actual and potential sources of supply as well as the actual resources being used and those that might substitute for them. He or she must also assess the organization's capacity to accommodate or to develop new sources of supply and to utilize alternative resources.

To a large extent, this capacity may correlate with how the organization perceives its consumers. *Consumers* may be perceived as "output" constituencies—that is, those who are the recipients of the services of the organization. Consumers can also be defined as "input" constituencies without whose contributions the agency's services would not be possible. When an agency organizes its clients into self-help groups or utilizes them as volunteers and aides with other, more dependent clients, it has redefined at least some of its output consumers as input constituencies.

Competitors are all those elements in the environment that compete for resources or for consumers. These may include alternative kinds of service providers who apply for the same limited source of government or private-sector financing. Competitors may also be from other sectors—researchers, public-interest groups, private practitioners—who compete for funds, public support, or even the use of facilities or newspaper space.

Effective program developers have often seen the potential of turning competitors into *collaborators*. Agencies that compete for scarce resources to hire staff might find it of benefit to try a number of alternative collaborative arrangements. For example, Agency A might "lend" a staff-member expert in family diagnosis to Agency B, which has neither the financial resources nor the experience to perform that kind of diagnosis. The staff member on loan would then operate as a member of the second agency's staff for an agreed-upon time period. An alternative might be to "out-station" staff members on the premises of another organization. Thus, for example, a rehabilitation worker from the state vocational rehabilitation agency or an SSI worker from the Social Security office might be out-stationed in a senior citizen's center two or three mornings a week.

How does this discussion relate to the topic of assessment? We might begin by examining where an agency or program fits in its task environment and then identifying the range of connections it has to elements in the environment. In effect, we would be using a *mapping technique,* not too different from the one described in the family space ecomap.

The instructions that follow provide an ecomapping exercise for staff and board members from one or more agencies. It can be used for training or program development. Consider trying the exercise yourself first. Nevertheless, you may have access to only part of the information you need. Who else has access to information? How might they be involved in the exercise? When?

Instructions for Task-Environment Mapping

(1) Begin by placing your agency or another one with which you are familiar in the center of Figure 2.5. Later, when you are more conversant with this tool, you may wish to locate an organization with which you are not familiar in the center, particularly if it is one whose programs or policies you are hoping

to influence. If you work in a large, multistructural organization, like a department of social services or a regional hospital, you might prefer to do the exercise with your work unit in the center. Alternatively, you might show the connections between designated units in the agency to elements in the organization's task environment. Use newsprint or a larger sheet of paper, if you wish; it will be easier to fill in.

(2) Now list those elements in the organization's or work unit's task environment in those boxes on the periphery of the square. It is possible that square design may not fit your situation. You may need a larger number of peripheral boxes for consumers and a smaller number for auspice providers, or vice versa. Feel free to modify the design to fit your situation.

(3) Just outside of those boxes, beyond the periphery, score each element in the task environment along two dimensions: importance (I) to your organization's survival or the achievement of its objectives, and amenability (A) to influence: +2 is very important or highly amenable; +1 is somewhat important or amenable; 0 suggests a rather neutral stance; –1 suggests the organization is hardly important or, in general, not very amenable to change; –2 indicates no importance whatsoever or little likelihood that it can be influenced. Designate your judgment by the symbols: I+2, I+1, I 0, I–1, I–2; and A+2, A+1, A 0, A–1, A–2.

(4) Now, in a different color of ink or pencil, add organizations that are not currently in the task environment but ones you think *will be* in the near future (anticipatory assessment), or that you think *should be* (normative assessment). Cross out those you feel will or should be irrelevant. Check those you wish to mark for change or for changed relationships. Rate the elements you have added for importance or amenability.

(5) You now have a map of what is, what is likely to be, and/or what ought to be. The next step is to decide what you and others with whom you work are going to do with the information. Are some of the elements in the task environment going to be targeted for a change-oriented intervention? Are there aspects of your own organization's procedures or activities that require changing?

(For a more comprehensive discussion of mapping the task environment, see Armand Lauffer, Lynn Nybell, Carla Overberger, Beth Reed, and Lawrence Zeff, *Understanding Your Social Agency*. Beverly Hills, CA: Sage Publications, 1977.)

Activity 2.3: Mapping Interorganizational Linkages

All social agencies are involved in a large variety of exchanges with collaborating organizations. You may wish to go beyond the confines of the task environment exercise to spell out the nature of the linkages with actual or potential collaborators. A partial inventory of potential linking mechanisms is found in the Glossary of Linkage Mechanisms that follows. Read it over. Then check those linking mechanisms that your agency or one with which you are concerned currently uses on the Inventory of Potentially Useful Linking Mechanisms (pp. 38-40). If you are aware of others that are not included on the list, add them.

Go over the inventory a second time. Which ones are currently underused or are not working well? Which of the linking mechanisms not currently being used ought to be? Check these in a different color. Are there some mechanisms the organization is mandated to use or will be required to use in the near future? Check these in a third color. You are now ready to complete the third mapping exercise.

Instructions for Interorganizational Linkage Exercises

(1) Locate an agency in the center circle of Figure 2.6.

(2) In the outer circle, write in the names of those organizations with which the agency is currently or may be involved in exchange relations. Identify those with which it is currently involved in one color, those with which it will probably be involved at some future date in a second color, and those with which it ought to be involved in a third color. If you need more space or are doing the exercise with other people, use a blackboard or a large sheet of newsprint.

(3) In the pie spaces between the inner and outer circles, indicate those linking mechanisms currently in effect, those that are likely to be, and those that ought to be. Use the same color coding you used for step 2. If you are interested in improving or

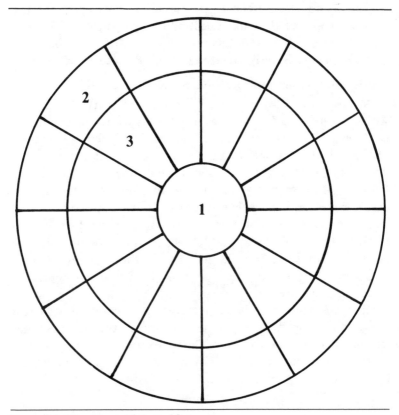

Figure 2.6 Interagency Linkage Map

1. Agency
2. Organizations with which Agency 1 is currently or potentially involved in exchange
   relationships.
3. Current or likely linking mechanisms.

modifying some of the existing linking mechanisms, circle or star them in the color used to indicate what "ought to be."

Your map may not be large enough to write in the full names of each of the types of linking mechanisms. An easy way to abbreviate them is by using the code from the Inventory you have just completed. Thus, A–5 would stand for case management, B–2 for co-location of staff, C-6 for Joint Public Relations, D-6 for Joint Budgeting, and soon.

(4) You are now ready to begin planning your intervention strategy. Ask yourself the following questions:

(a) Which linking mechanisms appear most often? Why? Which types of linking mechanisms am I most anxious to maintain or to increase?

(b) With which actual or potential collaborators are there the largest number or widest array of linking mechanisms? With which the fewest? Is the extent of the interdependence shown functional from the perspective of the agency in the center? How might this interdependence be modified, and to what end?

(c) What resources are needed to modify or expand these linkages?

GLOSSARY OF LINKAGE MECHANISM

This glossary is abstracted from Robert Rossi, Kevin Gilmartin, and Charles Dayton, *Agencies Working Together: A Guide to Coordination and Planning* (Beverly Hills, CA: Sage Publications, 1982). Refer to the glossary again in using the LINK game in Chapter 7.

Case conference. Staff from two or more agencies discuss the needs of clients they have in common informally and as needed.

Case consultation. Staff at one agency ask advice from staff at another agency regarding the needs of particular clients.

Case management. Staff at one agency are given responsibility for coordinating the services provided by several agencies to meet the needs of particular clients.

Client team. Staff from two or more agencies coordinate services to meet the needs of mutual clients through continuous and systematic interaction.

Co-location. Two or more agencies have staff and separate facilities at the same location; coordination of activities is optional.

Cross-referral network. Two or more agencies regularly refer clients back and forth, keeping track of their capabilities for providing services and monitoring the effectiveness of the referral process in meeting client needs.

Information clearinghouse. Staff at one location have responsibility for collection, classification, and distribution of information to several agencies, such as on labor market conditions, job openings, and client services available.

Interorganizational consultation and technical assistance. Experts from one agency provide consultation or technical assistance to another in return for similar or other benefits.

Joint budgeting. Two or more agencies coordinate the development of their annual budget so as to take into account how each agency's budgetary decisions affect the budgets of the other agencies.

Joint community needs assessment. The gathering and analysis of information on community needs by one agency, or by several agencies in cooperation.

Joint data-gathering or management information system. Collaborative efforts to gather data on client populations, resource capacities, or other areas of concern; can be manual or computer-based; data are accessible to those designated.

Joint fund raising. Organizations cooperate in funding drives, establishment of endowment funds, or in securing grants or contracts.

Joint funding (allocation). Organizations contribute dollars or in-kind resources for the funding of a collaborative project or for setting up an independent program.

Joint intake, screening, diagnosis. Two or more agencies develop a common system of processing new clients and diagnosing their needs to coordinate and improve the delivery of services from all relevant agencies.

Joint program design. Two or more agencies unite their efforts to plan and find resources for an effort.

Joint program evaluation. Two or more agencies unite their efforts to assess the effectiveness of an effort.

Joint program operation. Two or more agencies unite their efforts in the implementation of a program.

Joint public relations, news releases, and community education. Two or more organizations join efforts on behalf of a client population or their own resource needs, in educating the public or raising critical consciousness.

Joint standards and guidelines. Jointly arrived at or agreed-to practice standards, personnel standards, or action guidelines.

Joint training and staff development. Two or more organizations co-operate on training and development by co-sponsoring events, sharing successful programs, or trading their expertise.

Loaner staff. Staff from one agency are assigned to work (temporarily) under the direct supervision of another agency to carry out activities for that agency.

Purchase of services. One agency pays for specific services (such as outreach, intake, transportation, or diagnostic services) from another agency.

Sharing facilities or equipment. Permanent or ad hoc exchange of facilities like meeting rooms, offices, libraries; equipment like word processors, microcomputers, printing equipment, audio-visual equipment.

Staff outstationing. Staff from one agency are assigned to do their work in the facilities of another agency; coordination is necessary.

Standardizing procedures. Two or more agencies use the same procedures to respond to particular client needs.

Inventory of Potentially Useful Linking Mechanisms

A. Meeting Immediate Client Needs
- _____ 1. Cross-referrals
- _____ 2. Case consultation
- _____ 3. Case conferences
- _____ 4. Client teams
- _____ 5. Case management
- _____ 6. Joint intake, screening, diagnosis
- _____ 7. Case management by one agency

_____ 8. _____

_____ 9. _____

_____10. _____

B. Meeting Agency Personnel Needs

_____ 1. Staff outstanding

_____ 2. Co-location of staff

_____ 3. Loaner staff arrangements

_____ 4. Joint training and staff development

_____ 5. _____

_____ 6. _____

_____ 7. _____

C. Gathering, Exchanging and Disseminating Information

_____ 1. Joint community needs assessment of special studies

_____ 2. Information clearinghouse

_____ 3. Joint data-gathering or management information system

_____ 4. Joint program evaluation

_____ 5. Interorganizational consultation or technical assistance

_____ 6. Joint public relations, news releases, and community
          education

_____ 7. _____

_____ 8. _____

_____ 9. _____

D. Integrating Programs and Administration

_____ 1. Joint standards and/or guidelines

_____ 2. Sharing facilities and/or equipment

_____ 3. Joint program design

_____ 4. Joint program operation

_____ 5. Purchases of service

_____ 6. Joint budgeting

_____ 7. Joint fund raising

_____ 8. Joint funding (allocation)

_____ 9. Standardized procedures

_____10. _____

___11. _____

___12. _____

NEXT STEPS

Now that you've mastered three ecomapping techniques, consider how you will apply mapping tools to your own practice. Which of the three tools can you use pretty much as presented? With whom will you be using it? If you will be sharing the exercise with others, how and under what circumstances?

Feel free to photocopy any of the activity materials for use in introducing co-workers to the technique, in staff development or training programs, or in supervisory sessions with those staff members and volunteers with whom you work. Does any of the three activities require significant modification before it can be used? For example, would it pay to draw up some different kinds of family ecomaps that more properly describe the kinds of families with whom you or others in your agency are working? If you are concerned with relations between a planning agency and elements in its task environment, would you eliminate a number of linking mechanisms described in the glossary for activity 3? Would you substitute others?

Let's assume, for a moment, that none of the three activities quite fits your situation. What kinds of relations would an ecomapping process help you to understand better? I will list a few that students and colleagues have suggested to me. Why not add to the list?

- the relationships between an outreach worker, clients, and referral sources

- the relationships between a neighborhood association and a political and economic organization it wishes to influence

- the relationships between a child-care worker and all those who make it possible for her or him to go to work (foster parents, court officials, psychiatric consultations and others)

- _____

- _____

- _____

SUGGESTIONS FOR FURTHER READING

Charles Attneave, "Social Networks in the Unit of Attention," in P. J. Guerin, Jr. (ed.),
    Family Therapy. New York: Gardner Press, 1976.

Carel Germain, "An Ecological Perspective in Casework Practice." *Social Casework,* 54
    (June 1973): 232-330.

Irving Goffman, *The Presentation of Self in Everyday Life.* Garden City, NY: Doubleday,
    1959.

Ann Hartman, *Finding Families: An Ecological Approach to Family Assessment in
    Adoption.* Beverly Hills, CA: Sage Publications, 1979.

Armand Lauffer, *Getting the Resources You Need.* Beverly Hills, CA: Sage Publications,
    1982.

Armand Lauffer, *Doing Continuing Education and Staff Development.* New York:
    McGraw-Hill, 1978: Chapters 5 (Assessing Your Environment), 6 (Orchestrating
    Resources), and 9 (Building an Exchange Strategy Within Your Environment).

Armand Lauffer, *Social Planning at the Community Level.* Englewood Cliffs, NJ:
    Prentice-Hall, 1978: Chapters 5 (Resource Control and the Planner's Leverage), 10
    (Inter-Agency Linkages: Coordination at the Operational Level), and 13 (Natural and
    Extra-Professional Helping Systems).

James D. Thompson, *Organizations in Action.* New York: McGraw-Hill, 1967.

3. TASK ANALYSIS

Doin' What You Oughta

ILLUSTRATIONS FROM PRACTICE

Illustration 3.1: Deposits and Withdrawals From the Task Bank

When our personnel director came up with the idea of designing a "task bank" for the agency, I thought both the terminology and idea behind it peculiar. But as he explained how the banking process might work and what it could do for us, I began to see what he had in mind. Our situation at the time was desperate.

We were virtually out of resources. The combination of federal and state cutbacks meant we had to lay off 30 percent of our staff statewide, within six months. We'd already sustained a nine-month freeze on hiring, which left us with about 12 percent of our positions unfilled. Here's the situation we found ourselves in.

Some departments and some district offices were decimated. In some areas we had overqualified staff now responsible for doing tasks formerly assigned to clerical level personnel, because we couldn't hire secretaries. And in other places, professional tasks were left undone, because there were no pros to do them. In other areas, the full complement of staff was there, but we all knew that their productivity level wasn't where it had to be to respond to today's conditions. The idea of a "savings plan" in which we would put our scarce human resources into a bank, seemed at first ludicrous. That is, until I realized that you could also "withdraw" from the bank or borrow. You could also shift from one account to another. That's precisely what building a task bank is all about.

Illustration 3.2: The Butler Did It

We'd had time-and-motion problems around here for years. Everybody complained about the paperwork, and we didn't have enough time to see clients. It was about a year after we'd shifted to a more goal-oriented, somewhat behavioral orientation to treatment that Sally Margolis came up with the idea of using the same orientation to help organize their activities so as to have greater payoff for the clients and the agency. That meant having a clear idea of what in the things we did was "functional" and what was not.

Sally had just come back from a national conference in which she sat in on a workshop conducted by Sydney Fine, who I guess invented functional job analysis. Sally's our staff development specialist. Her enthusiasm and her expertise is what helped us carry through the process of analyzing everybody's job and figuring out where and when the task might be best performed, and by whom. It wasn't an easy process. But it did have great payoff.

The way it worked for us was that Sally and a small team (I was on it) interviewed everybody at the agency. We used a standard form and got everybody to spell out, in as precise terms as they could, the tasks that they performed. We learned from Fine's work that a task is the smallest unit of work that can be described. And to describe a task, you have to build it around an action verb, like "counsels," "records," "reports," or "refers." And then you have to build a sentence around that verb.

The sentence includes the following components: (1) who, (2) performs what action, (3) to whom or to what, (4) using what tools or methods, (5) to what end or for what purpose, (6) using what directions or under whose instructions. If you can spell it all out, what you've got is a "mapping" sentence. Here's an example from our agency's file of tasks. We call it a task bank.

The adoption worker writes letters to adoptive parents confirming agency decisions to place a child in their home and informing them of the necessary procedures in order to provide them with the information needed to begin the adoption process, under direction of the adoption supervisor.

Now it might be a bit hard to remember what all goes into the task statement. Sally had a trick sentence that you can never forget. Once you learn it, you will always know how to write a task statement.

> *The butler*
> *laces*
> *Mrs. Scarlett's tea*
> *with arsenic*
> *in order to do her in*
> *on behest of the upstairs maid.*

Once you've written your task statement, the next challenge is to identify the educational or work or skill-level prerequisites for entry level into a job in which that task must be performed. Then you design performance criteria so as to evaluate the level at which the task is being performed. Those two steps are useful for a couple of reasons. First, they allow us both to screen applicants and to evaluate their performance while on the job. It helps the supervisor and the worker jointly to evaluate the worker's achievement and his or her skill and knowledge deficits. Second, it creates a framework for staff development and training. After we were through with the process of identifying all the tasks that were being performed in the agency, it was possible for Sally to involve a committee of staff in specifying where they felt we all had deficits, or to spell out the levels of performance they thought we all ought to be striving for.

Actually, now that I think about it, task analysis did something else for us. It helped us to shift around tasks in relationship to competence and interest. As long as the tasks assigned to a work unit were performed, it didn't really matter who performed them. It became possible, therefore, for us to modify individual job descriptions. One of our foster care workers, for example, was really good at working the court system. She took on all the tasks related to the courts on behalf of all the workers in her unit. It saved everybody some time, gave her a lot of gratification and a lot of reward from the colleagues, and it made it possible for other workers to spend more time with foster parents and kids. Being goal-oriented, we discovered, wasn't only an individual process. It was a group process as well.

Illustration 3.3: A Community Organizer Does Case Management

I'm a community organizer, so when I got the assignment of designing a case management system for the agency, I thought that "task" had come at me from left field. Then I thought about it and I realized what a great opportunity it was to take the tool designed essentially for administrative purposes and to redesign it for community organization purposes. Here's what I did.

I used the same kind of mapping sentence you use to spell out the tasks that are to be performed by individual workers. In this case, however, I spelled out the tasks to be performed by staff in different organizations and then grouped those tasks in a way in which each agency knew what its functional responsibilities were to be. In order to make sure I wasn't imposing anything on anybody, I tested my model out with representatives of each of the agencies to be involved with us. They made some suggestions for changes and improvements.

The sticky point came when we had to identify performance criteria. That meant that each agency was going to have to agree to the criteria by which their involvement in case management process would be evaluated. It took a little give and take, and some horse trading. But I think we came up with a workable system.

I found the task analysis approach so useful that I'm planning to use it next month to work out the joint responsibilities to be shared between six agencies for a multicounty media campaign to highlight the needs of the elderly and the disabled.

TASK ANALYSIS: A SYSTEMS APPROACH

The idea behind the task-analytic methods we use today was developed in response to a problem that emerged early during

World War II. The Air Corps had been separated from the U.S. Army. A new service was established: the United States Air Force. It was necessary that the jobs and tasks assigned to each officer and enlisted man (or woman) be spelled out in clear language. The jobs would have to be functional, that is, they would have to articulate with each other and with the purposes or missions of the Air Force or the specific squadrons and units within it. It was necessary to know what each airman was to do. It was also necessary to know to whom he was responsible. As the analysis was carried out, it became clear that all personnel tasks tended to be performed in relationship to *things,* to *data,* and to *people.* Moreover, it was possible to order all these along some hierarchy of relative complexity or increasing responsibility.

Following World War II, a number of the people involved in the applications of task analysis to the military shifted to other government employ. Sydney Fine, one of the creators of the system, became involved in job, family, and test development work in the United States Training and Employment Services (USTES). In the early 1950s, he and his associates explored the application of the concepts developed for the Air Force to new occupational classification systems that might be developed on a theoretic rather than a strictly empirical basis. By the 1960s, it became clear that "functional job analysis" methods could be used for measuring general educational development and specifying the vocational preparation that might be useful in particular fields. Human resource shortages in both the scientific and the human service fields accelerated the need for a more comprehensive manpower analysis.

By 1970, Fine and his colleagues, now at the Washington-based Upjohn Institute for Employment Research, had put together a "task bank" for a typical statewide human service agency. The bank included virtually all the tasks that are performed in an agency, ranging from the clerical through the managerial and research tasks. Each was printed on a McBee card. You may not remember the old McBee cards. They predated the availability of inexpensive computers. Roughly 5×8 in size, McBee cards have small holes punched on all four sides. Each hole was number coded. If all these cards were in a box (the task bank) and you wanted to find out which tasks were performed by a senior adult outreach worker, you would need to know only the job's number. Assuming the outreach worker's number is 83, you would take a darning needle and stick it through number 83 on all the cards and lift up. Since all the cards with task descriptions not associated with the outreach worker would have hole 83 clipped out, the other cards would drop back in the box. All the task cards associated with job 83 would now be on your needle. One of the advantages of this system for storing and retrieving information is that you could, at any time, decide to reassign a task to another job number or job category.

With today's mini- and microcomputers and accompanying word processing equipment, McBee cards are hardly ever used. However, in those agencies experimenting with task analysis— especially if word-processing equipment is not available—McBee cards are still relatively easy to use. Most office supply stores have them on hand or can order them.

In the following pages, I will walk you through a simple exercise. You will be designing task statements and regrouping them into a job description. We will start with your own job. Once you have mastered the fundamentals, we will explore together how you might use task analysis for a variety of purposes in your own work setting. The exercise that follows differs somewhat from the format developed by Sydney Fine. I find it a bit easier to use.

ACTIVITIES

Activity 3.1: Doing Task Analysis Independently

Doing your own task analysis generally begins with an examination of your job description. A job description is a general statement of what a person does on the job. It is not a description of what he or she knows or at what level of skill a person should be performing. A functionally written job description should include all of the major tasks that are performed on the job. Unfortunately, most job descriptions are not written in this way, so that they may not serve their functions—as guides to the tasks that are to be performed. The sample job description that follows is a bit sketchy, but it will give you some idea of what might go into one.

Sample Job Description

The worker greets clients, obtains necessary case information from clients and from other relevant sources, and assess this information. He or she records this information on prescribed agency forms and sends it to the appropriate department, according to agency rule. The worker also informs clients of their rights and refers them to the appropriate department in the organization or to an external source of service.

Exercise 1: Examining the Sample Job Description

Before you begin working on your own job description, examine the sample we have provided you. Then proceed as follows:

(1) Underline all of the action verbs in blue pen or pencil (for example, "greets," "refers").
(2) In black ink, underline to whom or to what the action is referring. (for example, "clients," after the word "greets").
(3) Finally, with any color, circle those words that describe tools the worker might be using.

You may have noticed that "to whom" or "to what" the action refers is not always clear. Nor is it always clear what tools or methods are being used. Both are astute observations, and we will address them shortly. But before we do, you should complete Exercise 2.

Exercise 2: Writing Your Own Sample Job Description

In the blank box write up your own job description. If one already exists at the agency, use that. Otherwise write one up in your own words. Try to keep it to the single page provided. Do not forget to include action verbs. If you are finding it hard to work on your own job description, pick a colleague's job with which you are familiar. Use the blank form provided. You will be using another form later on. When you are finished, go back over your statement and underline all of the action verbs. Did you leave any out? If so, add sentences with action verbs that you think should have been included. Underline them.

Your Own Job Description

Exercise 3: Writing a Task Statement

These action verbs serve as a basis for writing task statements. For each action verb in the job description, it should be possible to generate a task statement. As defined in Illustration 3.2, a task statement includes information on six items: (1) who, (2) performs what action, (3) to whom or to what, (4) using what tools or methods, (5) to what end or for what purposes, (6) using what directions or under whose instructions.

On the form that follows, one action verb has been taken from the sample job description in order to show you how to write a task statement. (You will need more than a single copy of the task statement form. Feel free to photocopy or otherwise duplicate the form on page 52. For practice purposes, it might be good to start with five or six copies of the form.)

Sample Task Statement	
Title of Task: *Obtaining Case Information*	*Task Cluster: XXX*
Who	The child welfare worker
performs what action	obtains case information
to whom or to what	from clients
using what tools or methods	interviews by telephone, in the office or in home visit
to what end or for what purpose	to determine nature of service needed
using what directions or under whose supervision?	according to procedures found in the agency's manual and under guidance of the child welfare supervisor or the supervisor's designate.

Your Task Statement

Title of Task	*Task Cluster*

Who	1
performs what action	2
to whom or to what	3
using what tools or methods	4
to what end or for what purpose	5
using what direction or under whose supervision?	6

People_____   Ideas,   concepts _____   Materials _____

Entry-level requirements:	Performance criteria

Rating:

Importance Hi 5 4 3 2 1 Lo	Difficulty Hi 5 4 3 2 1 Lo
Frequency Hi 5 4 3 2 1 Lo	_____ Hi 5 4 3 2 1 Lo

Let us begin with the example of the task we identified as "obtaining case information." This is a task requiring work with people. Some tasks require working with "materials" almost exclusively (for example, filing, typing, addressing). Other tasks involve working with "ideas" (for example, designing a computer program, generating research hypotheses, preparing proposals). While there is certainly some work with ideas and with materials involved in "obtaining case information," the task is basically one in which interaction between people takes place.

We'll postulate that the task is performed in a family service agency. What basic expectations might we have of all persons performing this task? They might include fulfillment of certain entry-level requirements—completion of a B.A. degree in social work or psychology or their equivalent, empathy and under-standing, entry-level interviewing skills, and so on.

Most tasks can be done poorly or well, effectively or ineffec-tively. Once performance measures have been identified, it is possible to set performance standards, that is, to rate them along some agreed-upon scale. By performance standards we mean the level at which we expect the work to be done. This generally requires describing how we think the workers should perform the task. For example, if a worker's task is described as follows:

> receives, routes, transfers incoming telephone calls to the office requested by the caller, eliciting information as necessary to ascertain proper routing, using agency directories as required, in order to enable the caller to complete his call,

the performance standards might include the following:

- is tactful and pleasant with callers
- routes calls correctly and promptly
- operates equipment properly
- does not leave caller hanging or disconnect caller prior to indicating to caller that call cannot be completed at this point because of difficulties in routing the call.

Each of these might be ranked on a five-point scale, from acceptable to highly acceptable work, as follows:

5	4	3	2	1
high	better than average	acceptable	barely acceptable	un-acceptable

It is also possible to set some numerical measures for evaluating performance, such as:

- Over a two-week period, fewer than x number of complaints of incorrect routing will be made.
- Over a thirty-day period, no more than x number of complaints will be made that the worker was tactless or unpleasant with the caller.

Exercise 4: Clustering Tasks

There are many ways tasks can be clustered. One is to group them according to whether they reflect with people, ideas, or materials. These are rather broad categories, however. You may prefer to group the tasks you perform under functional categories. For example, a manager might group the tasks she performs under (1) orientation and training, (2) supervision of worker assignments, (3) work-flow planning, (4) data collection and reporting, and (5) performance evaluation. Any one of these clusters could include more discrete terms. For example, orientation and training might include:

- assessing worker performance
- establishing training objectives based on assessment of worker performance
- organizing orientation and training workshops
- arranging for experts to provide needed training

You have probably noticed that I did not write out each statement completely. This is not necessary when doing a preliminary clustering of tasks. We know, after all, *whom* we are discussing. Chances are that the answer to "under what direction or under whose supervision" will remain the same for each cluster. This may not be the case when you begin the task analysis process with other staff members in your organization. For now, I would like you to identify the major categories under which the tasks you perform tend to cluster. You can do this in one of two ways:

(1) Write down all the shorthand task statements you can in the following space for notes, and then look for some order or logic by which these might be clustered; or

(2) if you are pretty certain of the categories, put them down in the note section and add some notes about the tasks that might fall under each.

It is now time to summarize what you have done thus far. A blank worksheet appears on page 56. When you are ready, use the task summary worksheet on page 57. You will need five or six copies; feel free to photocopy the sample for your own purposes. To complete it, use the following procedures:

(1) Take one of the categories of work that you have just identified and write it in the upper left-hand corner of the task summary worksheet. Now, write all of the task statements that fall under that category of tasks. If there are more tasks than fit, use an additional sheet.

(2) Do the same for the other categories that you used for grouping your tasks. Feel free to make additional copies of the summary worksheets.

(3) Rate each of these tasks for importance. Use a scale of five to one, with five signifiying very important and one, not at all important.

Information gathered on the task summary workshop may be rewritten in the form of a job description.

Notes

Task Summary Worksheet

Category: _____

(Cluster Description)

Task	Importance	Frequency	Difficulty

**Activity 3.2: But How
About My Colleagues?**

"Okay," you may have developed some skill at describing task statements, and you have probably been surprised at what your job really looks like. But what do you do next?

First, you can share the experience you have just had with others at the agency. Feel free to duplicate the entire activity for (nonprofit) use as a training or assessment tool in your own agency. If you are going to use task analysis, you might want to explain to others that it is an assessment approach based on the following:

(1) use of a *standard (controlled) language* that introduces precision, clarity, and understanding to job descriptions;
(2) disaggregation of *jobs* into the series of *tasks* of which they are composed (tasks are the fundamental units of work);
(3) a *filing system* that makes it possible to inventory tasks and their definitions and combine them to describe existing or possible future job titles; and
(4) identification of tasks and their description in a *task definition* format.

The task definition is composed of the following components:

(1) use of a prescribed method for formulation of *task statements;*
(2) division of all work activity into three *functional areas* (people, data, things) that encompass what workers do in the entire world of work;
(3) ranking of the work functions on standard *worker function scales* for each of the three areas, to clarify requisite functional level of performance; and
(4) derivation of precise *performance standards, training needs*, and *worker qualifications* for each task from the task statement and worker function scales.

This approach can be used for supervision, the evaluation of worker performance, training and recruitment, and organizational analysis. As a supervisory tool, it (1) provides the supervisee and supervisor with an opportunity to clarify each worker's job, and (2) provides both with an opportunity to arrive at some agreement about the level of performance expected.

Supervisors have found that good job descriptions, especially those derived from task analysis, may be utilized to improve a work unit's function by increasing the clarity and precision of job descriptions. Misunderstandings are prevented when points of potential disagreement over job definitions and responsibilities are explicated. TA also provides a basis for mutual bargaining and negotiations between staff and line personnel.

As an evaluative tool, task analysis provides the supervisor with standards for assessing what the worker does in relationship to what he or she should be doing, and a guide against which the worker can compare his or her own accomplishments in relation to an agreed-upon norm.

As a training or recruitment device, task analysis establishes clear statements about the tasks that workers are to perform, a means of assessing where current staff and potential recruits are in relationship to those norms, and a way of spelling out in detail the requirements of the job.

Learning objectives for staff development or in-service training can be formulated in accordance with the task statements and the standards associated with each. These standards include expected levels of performance as well as required levels of skill or competence prior to entry into a particular job.

As a tool for organizational analysis and redesign, task analysis provides information necessary for job restructuring so as to make most efficient use of available human resources, and access to information on the part of all members of the agency staff for use in problem solving.

Fine and Wiley's People Function Scale, presented in Table 3.1, provides a systematic categorization of functions to be considered in task assessment analysis.

TABLE 3.1   People Function Scale

The arabic numbers assigned to definitions represent the successive levels of this ordinal scale. The *A, B,* and *C* definitions are variations on the same level. There is no ordinal difference between *A, B,* and *C* definitions on a given level.

Level	Definition
	Taking Instructions—Helping
1A	Attends to the work assignment, instructions, or orders of supervisor. No immediate response or verbal exchange is required unless clarification is needed.
	Serving
1B	Attends to the needs or requests of people or to the expressed or implicit wishes of people. Immediate response is involved.
	Exchanging Information
2	Talks to, converses with, and/or signals people to convey or obtain information, or to clarify and work out details of an assignment within the framework of well-established procedures.
	Coaching
3A	Befriends and encourages individuals on a personal, caring basis by approximating a peer or family-type relationship either in a one-to-one or small-group situation; gives instruction, advice, and personal assistance concerning activities of daily living, the use of various institutional services, and participation in groups.
	Persuading
3B	Influences others in favor of a product, service, or point of view by talks or demonstrations.
	Diverting
3C	Amuses to entertain or distract individuals and/or audiences or to lighten a situation.
	Consulting
4A	Serves as a source of technical information and gives such information or provides ideas to define, clarify, enlarge upon, or sharpen procedures, capabilities, or product specifications (e.g., informs individuals/families about details of working out objectives such as adoption, school selection, and vocational rehabilitation; assists them in working out plans and guides implementation of plans).
	Instructing
4B	Teaches subject matter to others or trains others, including animals, through explanation, demonstration, and test.
	Treating mmm mmm 10.53

TABLE 3.1 (Continued)

Level	Definition

Treating

4C   Acts on or interacts with individuals or small groups of people or animals who need help (as in sickness) to carry out specialized therapeutic or adjustment procedures. Systematically observes results of treatment within the framework of total personal behavior because unique individual reactions to prescriptions (chemical, physical, or behavioral) may not fall within the range of prediction. Motivates, supports, and instructs individuals to accept or cooperate with therapeutic adjustment procedures when necessary.

Supervising

5   Determines and/or interprets work procedure for a group of workers; assigns specific duties to them (delineating prescribed and discretionary content); maintains harmonious relations among them; evaluates performance (both prescribed and discretionary) and promotes efficiency and other organizational values; makes decisions on procedural and technical levels.

Negotiating

6   Bargains and discusses on a formal basis as a representative of one side of a transaction for advantages in resources, rights, privileges, and/or contractual obligations, "giving and taking" within the limits provided by authority or within the limits provided by authority or within the framework of the perceived requirements and integrity of a program.

Mentoring

7   Works with individuals having problems affecting life adjustment in order to advise, counsel, and/or guide them according to legal, scientific, clinical, spiritual, and/or other professional principles. Advises clients on implications of analyses or diagnoses made of problems, courses of action open to deal with them, and merits of one strategy over another.

Source. Reprinted from Sydney A. Fine and Wretha W. Wiley, *An Introduction to Functional Job Analysis* (Kalamazoo: W. E. Upjohn Institute for Employment Research, 1971), with permission. This scale is one of three scales; the other two are the Things and the Data Function Scales.

OTHER POTENTIAL APPLICATIONS

Although, as our discussion has shown, task analysis has been used primarily as a tool for job design and development within an organization, there are a number of other potential applications. For example, a simplified version of task analysis might be used with a family in therapy, particularly where responsibilities for certain behaviors (such as cleaning house, shopping, initiating recreation activities) are either heavily lodged in a single person, or unclear in terms of expectations. Members of a political or social action coalition might use task analysis as away of specifying responsibility and coordinating goal-oriented behavior. A community organizer or social planner, as in the third case example at the beginning of this chapter, might use task analysis as a way of specifying the functional responsibilities assigned to different organizations involved in some exchange or networking process. What other applications can you think of?

SUGGESTIONS FOR FURTHER READING

Michael Debloois and Raymond C. Melton, *Functional Task Analysis: The Training Module.* Tallahassee: Florida Department of Education, 1974.

Sydney Fine and Wretha W. Wiley, *An Introduction to Functional Job Analysis.* Kalamazoo, MI: W. E. Upjohn Institute for Employment Research, 1971.

Armand Lauffer, "Working with Volunteers," *Resources for Child Placement.* Beverly Hills, CA: Sage Publications, 1977.

U.S. Department of Health, Education and Welfare, *The National Task Bank.* Washington, DC: Social and Rehabilitation Service, Office of Manpower Development and Training, 1972.

end of chapter 5.64

4. THE NOMINAL GROUP TECHNIQUE
Setting an Action Agenda

ILLUSTRATIONS FROM PRACTICE

Illustration 4.1: Some Help for Self-Help

The first meeting was a disaster. I had heard of Phyllis Silverman's work in organizing widow-to-widow groups in the Boston area[1] and thought it would be a good idea to organize a similar group here. Having been widowed only two years ago, I had empathy for many of our clients who were in a similar situation. I asked each of the other caseworkers at the agency to refer clients to a new group I was forming. At the first meeting, eleven women came. They ranged in age from 45 to 63.

Since I knew their life circumstances were all a bit different, I thought I'd initiate the process by talking about my own widowhood. I talked and everyone listened politely, but when I tried to get other people to volunteer their feelings or their experiences, it was a disaster. Nobody said anything. Finally, Monica Merle, an attractive woman in her mid-fifties, spoke up. But she wasn't sure what to say either. I had a feeling she was just talking to fill the silence, and in fact trying to help me out of my difficulty. Some situation. Here I'd convened the group to help them, and one of the members was trying to help me.

1. See Phyllis R. Silverman, *Mutual Help Groups* (Beverly Hills, CA: Sage Publications).

Following Monica's comments, a few women raised their hands and asked what the purposes of the group were. I said a few trite things about all of us having experienced similar losses, and how we go through different stages of grief until we're able to cope with the world around us again, and how I thought it would be helpful if we shared our coping experiences. I don't think anyone was really convinced. I was beginning to doubt the value of the group myself. But at least everyone agreed to come back the following week to try again. As she was putting her coat on, Monica asked if it was okay if she were to call me later in the week. She had one or two ideas about how to get the group moving. I was delighted.

"You know," she explained on the phone a few days later, "I've been active in church groups all my life. I've worked on a lot of committees and I always find that they have a difficult time focusing in on what they should be dealing with. Some people take the lead and everybody else gets squeezed out. I've had a lot of success with a technique that gets everybody involved. Here's how it works." I listened.

It sounded good. We decided to use it at the next meeting. This is what we did.

When the group was assembled, I explained that while I know each one of us was a unique person, we've probably all shared similar problems as widows, problems that are not only difficult to deal with, but hard to talk about with strangers. "Would you mind," I asked, "if I pass out these 3 × 5 cards? Take as many as you think you'll need.

"On each, jot down a situation that has become especially hard for you at the onset of widowhood. Don't write your name. We'll keep this anonymous. Later we'll see if we have problems in common."

I gave everybody four or five minutes to write. Then I collected the cards and invited everyone to have some coffee and doughnuts. Monica and I sorted out the cards and found that they tended to fall into four categories: (1) moments of uncontrollable grief, (2) difficulty in handling children's behavior (including adult children), (3) management problems (including financial management), and (4) role problems (not knowing how to deal with old friends or not knowing how to respond to unattached males). I wrote the categories across the chalkboard at the front of the room. Under each category I taped the appropriate cards.

I started off by reading all the cards under a given category and asking people if they felt that several of the cards talked about problems that were similar enough that we might consolidate them. Under the "grieving" category, for example, we started off with sixteen cards and were able to consolidate down to five by doing some modest rewriting and removing the overlaps. When we'd finished the four categories, I asked each woman to take a minute or less to talk about those problems she thought it might be helpful for us to deal with together. It didn't have to be a problem she had written. It was only important that she felt the group could be helpful with it. I then gave everyone a chance to talk round-robin style.

I was amazed at how easy it was for everybody to talk and how attentive the other women were. When everyone had finished, I remarked on how honest and open everyne had been. Because it was hard for us to deal with all problems at once (just as it had been hard for them to deal with all these problems at once in their own personal lives), we would have to prioritize, choosing those issues we should address first.

I then gave everyone a chance to vote on two items under each category. When we were all finished, it was clear that some items had higher priority than others. Next, I asked them whether they wanted to work on those issues that had garnered the most votes or whether they thought it might be best to deal with the issues category by category. Everyone agreed that it would be best to deal with those problems that had the most votes, regardless of categories.

Well, we had our agenda. It wasn't long before we had a clear idea of our purpose and how we could be helpful to each other. The amazing thing about this process is that it gave everyone a chance to contribute equally, regardless of their previous group experience.

Illustration 4.2: Setting Priorities at the Neighborhood Level

We just seemed to be getting nowhere. Every meeting ended in a jumble of confusion and hostility. Mrs. Carmichael, who was a mighty powerful woman, seemed to be doing most of the talking. People were afraid to raise their voices against her. All but Lettie Benedict, who had once worked as a secretary in the mayor's office. Because of her reputed "connections," the fireworks between them were something to watch. But it kept almost everyone else out of the dialogue, if you could call it that.

I shared my problem with Mark Habib, an experienced community organizer, also on our staff. "Look," he said to me. "Why not use the nominal group technique? You know what the problems are in your neighborhood, at least the general categories. Before the next meeting get yourself a big pad of newsprint.

"On the top of each sheet, put the title of one problem category, like 'street repair,' or 'muggings,' or 'retail gouging.' Then hang up the sheets around the walls of the clubhouse where you meet.

"When you have your next meeting, give everybody a magic marker and have them go up to the wall and write their action suggestions under each category."

It worked like a charm. Everybody seemed to have a good time writing. Some people even started correcting other people's grammar and spelling. People talked informally about the suggestions they thought were good ones, and those they thought were way out. After a while I asked everyone to sit down. I asked Mrs. Carmichael to read each of the suggestions made under each category. If there were overlaps, I asked Lettie to fix them up by consolidating them into shorter statements while Mrs. Carmichael went over to read the next set of categories.

When we were all through, I told them now it was time to express their opinions for real. Everybody would be given thirty seconds to convince us about the action steps we should take first as a neighborhood group. They could try to convince us on the basis of how important a problem was or on the basis of how easy it was to solve. No sense in working on things that weren't going to yield up any solutions. Now you might think that thirty seconds isn't very much time. But you'd be amazed at how much you can say in thirty seconds if you really think about it. One of the problems with these people was they would talk without thinking. Talk about being amazed. Were they ever amazed at how much they got done in less than a half hour!

We then voted on the action steps we wanted to pursue as an organization during the next month or two. Again, talk about being amazed. There was an incredible amount of consensus. We decided on three concrete action steps. True, some people were disappointed that their priorities were low on the totem pole. But at least everybody'd had a fair chance to make a contribution and everybody'd had the same chance to vote. "This won't mean that we can't work on any other issues," I explained at the end of the meeting. "We've decided what we're going to do first. We'll have a chance to set priorities again next month, after we've had an opportunity to take stock on how we're doing on what we decided tonight."

A TECHNIQUE FOR NONGROUP GROUPS

If you have participated in as many meetings as I have, you have probably noticed two interrelated phenomena. People do a lot of talking, but they don't seem to be able to make decisions easily. Or only a few people do a lot of talking, and tend to carry the group because of their charisma, their ability to think on their feet, or the status they hold in the organization or the community. When decisions do get made, they are often the result of a "groupthink" process in which only a relatively small number of ideas are ever fully explored, and in which a decision is made because it seems to be the easiest decision to make.

The "problem of decisions" is even greater when people of diverse backgrounds, who may have a little in common with each other or who have relatively little experience in group processes, are brought together to take action or to set policies or to decide on procedures. The Delbecq-Van de Ven-Gustafson nominal group technique (NGT)[2] and its variations seem tailor-made for these situations. The technique was developed while Delbecq and Van de Ven were teaching at Wisconsin in the mid-1960s. It was found to be exceptionally useful in work with citizen groups involved in community action programs. The technique has long been known to trainers and staff developers.

Delbecq and Van de Ven point out that NGT is useful in (1) problem exploration, (2) knowledge exploration, (3) preliminary review, (4) design and implementation activities, and (5) evaluation and review activities. At any of these stages in the planning and decision-making process, NGT can be used to assess what is, and what is likely to be, or what ought to be. It is a matter of phrasing the initial question. For example, you might ask people to begin by jotting down the major problems to be addressed by the organization or the community; or you could ask them to list their educational needs. You might even ask them to list the resources available to deal with those problems and needs, as well as those that currently are not available. These are here-and-now items.

You might also ask them to do the same in anticipation of a given situation two or three years hence. For example, when it became clear that institutions for the developmentally disabled and for the mentally ill would all but close within a two-year period, we (a team from the University of Michigan) asked a group of mental health practitioners and hospital administrators to project the needs that formally institutionalized patients would

---

2. André L. Delbecq, Andrew H. Van de Ven, and David H. Gustafson, *Group Techniques for Program Planning: A Guide to Nominal Groups and Delphi Processes* (Glenview, IL: Scott, Foresman, 1976).

have. We also asked them to spell out the problems that communities would have to face in dealing with those needs. This led to the development of an action agenda intended to prepare both families and communities to deal with anticipated future problems. With another group of professionals, we used the nominal group technique to generate a normative model. We asked them to spell out the components of an effective community placement system and the resources needed to establish that system. We then asked them to prioritize along two dimensions: salience or importance, and feasibility.

You may wonder why NGT is referred to as a "nominal group" technique. This is to distinguish the process from more interactive group processes. It is not necessary to use NGT in an ongoing group. It can be used as a one-shot activity in a setting in which people who are not members of a group are nonetheless required to set priorities or to generate ideas. Their actions are only "nominally" group actions.

NGT is a structuring process. It is intended to generate outcomes quickly and systematically. It is no substitution for bargaining, posturing, or the negotiations process that often takes place in interactive groups. It is a special purpose technique. You would not expect to use it at staff meetings on a regular basis. But you might use it to deal with a specific issue or complex of issues. It is most useful when you are concerned with the implications of assessment for judgmental decision making.

It is a creative process that presumes either a lack of agreement at the outset or an incomplete state of knowledge concerning the nature of the problem or the components that must be included in generating a successful solution. It is a way of increasing the likelihood that heterogeneous group members can pool their judgments and, in so doing, invent or discover a satisfactory course of action. It is a technique that can be used for tapping the judgments of agency administrators and staff, outside resource experts, agency clients, community members, and others with different backgrounds, perspectives, or positions.

NGT has also been widely adopted as a technique for involving clients and other consumers in problem identification. It does not require their ongoing participation, but it does assure their input into the decision-making process. It trusts their judgments and it enables them to share their expertise with that of professionals and others.

According to Van de Ven and Delbecq, the advantages of NGT over other processes is that it generates consistency in decision making and reduces variations in inputs between members and leaders.[3] Participants are rewarded and reinforced through their sense of having achieved the task or the challenge set before them. Because individuals have an opportunity to think through and write down their ideas, there is a tendency for these ideas to be problem-centered, specific, and of relatively high quality.

The fact that both the assessment and the decision-making processes are structured generates greater tolerance for nonconforming and incompatible, or conflicting ideas, because everyone has an equal opportunity to express those ideas without interruption during the search and choice periods of decision making. The very nature of this structured process guarantees equality of participation among members, reducing the dominance of certain individuals. Finally, the NGT meetings tend to conclude with a perceived sense of group closure and accomplishment, as well as an interest in the future phases of the problem-solving process. Delbecq et al. (1976: 14) summarize the process of decision making in NGT:

(1) a solitary generation of ideas in writing;

(2) round robin feedback from group members to record each idea in a terse phrase on a flip chart;

(3) the discussion of each recorded idea for clarification and evaluation;

(4) individual voting and priority ideas with a group decision being mathematically derived through rank-ordering or rating.

3. Andrew H. Van de Ven and André L. Delbecq, "The Effectiveness of Nominal, Delphi, and Interacting Group Decision Making Processes," unpublished manuscript, no date.

4. André L. Delbecq, Andrew H. Van de Ven, and David H. Gustafson, *Group Techniques for Program Planning*, p. 14.

ACTIVITIES

Two activities follow. First I will guide you through a simplified—and probably the most popular—way to use the nominal group technique. In the second activity, I will introduce you to a more complex variation that I call the "team planning technique" (TPT). I developed the TPT as part of an extensive training project for middle managers in Israel's National Insurance Institute. I subsequently used it for problem solving in settlement houses, with neighborhood associations, in public welfare bureaucracies in both Israel and the United States. It can easily be adapted for use in a variety of settings.

Activity 4.1: Using the
Nominal Group Technique

Begin by deciding on what context and for what purposes you will be using NGT. A partial inventory of possible uses follows. Add some of your own. Then go back and decide for which purpose and in what setting you will use it.

- with agency decision makers in setting budget or program priorities
- with staff at the agency to identify staff development needs or job satisfaction problems
- with community members in setting an action agenda
- with clients in order to identify services they are most interested in receiving from the agency
- with a group of experts on community placement to establish a normative model that they should be aiming toward
- _____
- _____
- _____
- _____
- _____

Invite people to a meeting or attend a meeting at which assessments and decisions can be made. Follow the four steps listed above. Now decide whether you want to use the open-ended method described by the organizer of the widow-to-widow group in the first vignette or whether you would prefer a more structured format in which categories are predetermined (as in Illustration 4.2).

Now go to it. Depending on the size of the group, the process will probably take you between forty-five minutes and two hours. Make sure you have enough time. Also, be sure to let the participants know what you and others intend to do with the results, or what *they* may be expected to do after they have generated their assessments and made their judgments.

Activity 4.2: The Team Planning Technique (TPT)

In the team planning technique, NGT is integrated with aspects of task analysis. TPT can be mastered by people who have had no experience with task analysis. In many respects it serves as a foundation for task analysis, particularly when participants focus on needs or problems that are directly related to the performance of work-related tasks. Those familiar with task analysis will find many of the thought processes inherent in TPT compatible with what they have already learned. The stages of the TPT are summarized in the boxed table that follows.

The instructions that follow provide guidance for identifying work-related/learning needs as well as work-related problems, and for designing an instructional program to deal with those needs and problems. A similar procedure might be used for developing work-related program objectives and listing the tasks that must be performed in order to achieve those objectives. TPT can be modified for work with small groups (four to five people). As described in the following pages, it presumes two or more small groups (each composed of up to nine people).

TPT includes individual, small group, intergroup and large group activities. It begins with the division of all participants into small groups of five to nine people. Participants work in these groups from Stage 1 through Stage 3. Stage 4 requires work in intergroup subcommittees. During Stage 5, participants convene in one large group. They are back together in their teams again during Stages 6 and 7 and end in the large group at Stage 8.

The requisite small groups of five to nine need not be convened especially for this exercise. They may be composed of the natural groups that already exist, such as foster care or adoption units in a public welfare agency, neighborhood action teams in a community development corporation, or staff members in a group living facility. Intergroup activities would require movement of representatives of each natural group. Large group activities might involve the entire staff of an agency, a department, or a branch.

Read through the instructions once. On first reading, you may find them somewhat complex. Read them again, this time stage by stage. Stop and think through what you might do as the convenor at each stage. Work up a scenario in your mind. Imagine the kinds of issues or questions that might be addressed in each small group, during the intergroup sessions, or in the large group meetings. Then go on to the next stage. It is important to be well prepared before taking on the leadership of any group process.

Instructions for the participants will be given in the left-hand column under the heading of each of the stages of the team planning technique. Notes to the convenor or process leader of TPT will be given in the right-hand column. The notes for adapting TPT to specific work-related situations, which follow, may be helpful. Go back over the instructions for participants and think through the adaptations that would have to be made to use TPT in your own work setting. If you do decide to use TPT, you might want to discuss those adaptations with others whose support will be needed to assure that the process works well and that the outcomes of the process will, in fact, make a difference to those who participate in the exercise.

Stages of the Team Planning Technique

Approximate Time Needed

1. Need and Problem Definition
   a. identifying needs and problems — 15 minutes
   b. listing all the important dimensions
      of the needs and problems — 30 minutes
2. Sharing Information on Needs and Problems
   a. listing the group's collective needs
      and problems by category — 15 minutes
   b. clarifying the needs and problems listed — 30 minutes
3. Consolidating and Selecting from
   the Needs and Problems Listed — 2 hours
4. Integrating the Work of Each Team — 30 minutes
5. Priority Setting — 1 hour
6. Turning Needs and Problems Statements
   into Objectives — 2 hours
7. Working Out the Action Plan
   a. spelling out the content of instruction — 30 minutes
   b. spelling out organizational actions
      to be taken — 30 minutes
8. Ratifying the Objectives and Their
   Order of Priority — 1 hour

The entire process, from Stage 1 through Stage 8, takes about nine hours. The actual time spent on each stage can be modified when working straight through (as during a specially scheduled workshop or retreat). It might be well to work through Stage 5 in one sitting (with appropriate rest and eating breaks). This takes about five hours. Stages 6 through 8, which take about four hours, might be conducted on another day.

If the TPT is to be used during regular work hours, other scheduling arrangements will have to be worked out. A workable schedule might be as follows: Stages 1 and 2 (one and one-half hours), Stage 3 (two hours), Stage 4 (intergroup activity to be scheduled for about one-half hour), Stage 5 (one hour), Stage 6 (two hours), Stages 7 and 8 (two hours).

Stage 1: Needs and Problem Definition
a. *Identifying Needs and Problems (about 15 minutes)*

Instructions for Participants

Think about your own learning and development needs in relation to your job or career interests. Using 3 × 5 cards, record up to three of those learning needs, one per card.

Start each card by writing: "I need to learn . . ." and then add "about" or "how to," concluding with what it is you want to learn.

> *Examples*: "I need to learn how to conduct a staff meeting"; "I need to know more about how policy decisions are made in my agency."

Keep your needs statement simple, listing only *one need per card* ("I want to learn how to conduct a staff meeting and to involve staff in decision making" spells out two needs instead of one, even though they may be interrelated). Focus on your need, not the organization's. Once you have completed your needs statements, use up to three cards to describe three different problems at work. Again, list one problem per card. Focus on problems that affect how work is done and its impact on achievement of the organization's mission or its ability to maintain itself.

Notes to the Convenor

Convene participants in groups of five to nine or use natural work groupings in the organizational setting. If you have several groups working at the same time in a large room, arrange for each to work on a table of its own. Have the necessary number of 3 × 5 cards and pens or pencils available to each.

Go over the instructions, making sure that people understand the differences between needs and problems and that they keep their statements simple.

Be available to help individuals if they are having problems.

If some participants finish before others, ask them to go over their cards to make sure that they are written in such a way that they convey the writer's meaning.

Remember that these are individual statements. Participants should work independently, even if they are seated close to each other.

Instructions for Participants

Once you have completed your needs statements, use up to three cards to describe three different problems at work. Again, list one problem per card. Focus on problems that affect how work is done and its impact on achievement of the organization's mission or its ability to maintain itself.

> *Examples*: "There is serious problem of morale in my work unit"; "Other managers in my branch feel anger toward the organization because they feel left out of the policymaking process"; "Intake workers route new clients to the wrong office at least 25 percent of the time."

Keep your problem statement simple, listing only one problem per card. Focus on the work-related problem, not on your own learning needs, even though you may need to learn how to deal with that problem more effectively. Use your convenor as a consultant if you are having difficulties.

Notes to the Convenor

Special note: It is not necessary for participants to work on both needs and problems. Should you prefer to focus on *either* needs or problems, modify the instructions for Stage 1a accordingly, and then make similar modifications for subsequent stages.

b. Listing All the Important Dimensions of the Needs and Problems (about 30 minutes)

Select the need cards and the problem cards that are most important to you. Be certain to select at least *one need* and *one problem* card. On the back of each of these cards, spell out all the dimensions of the need or problem that you can think of.

Be available as needed. Help participants think through the dimensions of the need or problem that they feel require action. In effect, they are taking a general statement of need or of a problem and spelling it out in more concrete terms.

Instructions for Participants

For example, if you need to learn "how to conduct a meeting"; you might consider the following dimensions: making up the agenda, how to write the protocol, involving participants in the discussion, getting people to think about the issues to be discussed and preparing for the discussion in advance, resolving conflicts, and making decisions.

For example, if you are concerned about the problem of morale, you might consider the following dimensions: whether the problem is felt by everyone in your unit, what motivates people to work and to what extent they are reinforced for doing a job well, the relationships between workers, and how morale effects performance on the job.

Be sure to work on those needs or problems that are most important to you first. If you have enough time, work on the others as well. Use the convenor as a consultant if you need help.

Notes to the Convenor

Prepare for Stage 2. As you move from group to group, examine the needs and problems statements that participants have recorded. Look for emerging patterns. It is your task to find those patterns. You may find the following categories of needs and problems arenas suggestive. Use them if they seem to fit, but do not be limited by them. It is possible that none of the needs or problems identified will fit some of the arenas suggested, in which case you might have to drop some of and others.

Management-Related Arenas
  Morale/group cohesion
  Authority/power
  Communication
  Procedures
  Staff management
  Supervision

Resource-Related Arenas
  Resource acquisition
  Resource allocation
  Budgeting (money, time, other resources)

Program/Service-Related Arenas
  Availability and accessibility
  Effectiveness
  Efficiency
  Accountability
  Comprehensiveness
  Coordination

Policy-Related Arena
  Locus of decision making
  Appropriateness

Stage 2: Sharing Information on Needs and Problems
*a. Listing the Group's Collective Needs
and Problems by Category (about 15 minutes)*

Instructions for Participants

Now that you have completed your definitions of needs and problems, it is time to find out how others in your group perceive their own needs and the organization's problems, and to share your own perceptions.

While your were completing Stage 1b, I, the convenor, was developing a set of categories for grouping needs and problems statements. We will be referring to these as "practice arenas." The title for each of these arenas has been written on a large sheet of paper (one title per sheet) that I have left at your table.

Select one person to act as "team leader" and one person to act as the "recorder." The leader asks each person at the table, one at a time, to read those of his/her needs he/she considers most important. The recorder writes out the needs statement on the large sheet of paper (without the star) that properly classifies the arena under which it falls. He or she uses the same color marking pen as used for the heading on the sheet.

> *For example,* knowing about "how policies in the organization are made" would fit under

Notes to the Convenor

Before participants can start Stage 2, you will have to have provided them with the categories under which they can group their needs and problems statements. Use those suggested under Stage 1b or others that fit your situation better.

It is likely that some of the same arenas will fit both the needs and problems statements that individuals have recorded. If this is the case, use them as headings twice, once for needs and once for problems. Put an asterisk (*) next to the title used for the recording of problems statements.

Put the headings you have decided on at the top of large sheets of paper (24 × 30 sheets of newsprint, for example). Prepare a set for each team so that participants can use them for Stage 2.

the "program and policy development" arena. It would be written in black.

There should be no interruption or discussion by other group members as the person whose turn it is reads out his or her needs statement(s). Only those needs cards that have dimensions on the reverse side should be read. Read only what is on the front of the card.

As soon as one person has finished, the leader asks the next person to read his/her statement(s) while the recorder once again writes it down.

b. Clarifying the Needs and Problems Listed (about 15 minutes)

At this point, the leader again calls on each person to speak, one at a time. When it is your turn to speak, you may take up to two minutes to speak about one of the needs or problems statements you contributed, or four minutes to talk about two of them. You may not speak about someone else's contribution or interrupt when someone else is speaking.

Be available as needed. Circulate.

When you are speaking, refer to the dimensions of the need or problem that you wrote on the back of the card and indicate why you think this issue should be

Instructions for Participants   *Notes to the Convenor*

addressed in the training program, or by the organization more broadly. If you go over your allotted time, the leader will ask you to stop talking, so it is important for you to organize your thoughts and to present them clearly.

Stage 3: Consolidating and Selecting from the Needs and Problems Listed (about 2 hours)

Once Stage 2 is completed and everyone has had a turn, it is time to consolidate those statements that seem to overlap or duplicate each other, and to select from them those the group feels are most important. Those persons who were selected to serve as leaders and recorders may continue to play those roles. Alternatively, you may select other people to perform the requisite tasks.

Be available as needed. Circulate.

Collectively, you may not have less than twelve or more than eighteen needs and problems listed.

You may use any procedure you like so that everyone has an opportunity to make an input. This is now a collective enterprise. The team may rewrite any of the needs or problems statements to reflect the interests of the largest number. Rewriting may be done through participation of all group members or by delegating responsibility to those most concerned.

Stage 4: Integrating the Work of Each Team (about 30 minutes)

Instructions for Participants

While the recorder in each group is rewriting notes, each of the other members of the group takes one of the large sheets of newsprint on which the needs and problems were written.

If there are six other members of the group, each member takes either a "needs" or a "problems" sheet reflecting a particular arena. Should the number of team members and categories (arenas) under which needs and problems were listed not be identical, it may be necessary for more than one person to work on one sheet or for one person to work on two sheets.

Take the sheet for which you are responsible and meet with the persons from the other small groups who are responsible for the same arena. You are now working on an "interdepartmental level," in subcommittees. It is each subcommittee's job to make up a new sheet which lists the items from all of the groups. Eliminate duplications and overlaps through consolidating or rewriting where appropriate. But do not attempt to eliminate or reduce the number of items for any other reason. Post the completed sheets on the wall.

The needs statements should precede the problem statements.

Notes to the Convenor

This is an opportunity to rewrite the needs and problems statements clearly and to make sure that similar style and language is used throughout.

Help the interdepartmental groups rewrite or consolidate as indicated. Be available as needed, but do not do the work for each group.

Stage 5: Priority Setting (about 50 minutes)

Before proceeding, post each integrating group's list of needs or

Instructions for Participants

problems. There should be as many lists as there were problem or need arenas discussed. Post the lists at the front of the room where you will be conducting a general meeting and then convene everyone. Proceed as follows:

This is the first of two opportunities we will have to make some decisions as a total group. Notice that we have posted the need (problem) issues that the integration groups selected from among those discussed in your work groups. I will read the items on each list. If you have any questions about their meaning, please hold them until after I've finished a list. If I can't answer them, one of the members of the integration group that worked on the list in question should be able to.

a. Explain the process you will all be following.
b. Read each list, item by item, seeking clarification where needed.
c. Conduct a round-robin discussion.
d. Rank order items on each list through a voting procedure.
e. Decide which items are to be carried over to Stage 6.

READ EACH LIST

Now, let's find out why some people feel strongly about certain items. Each of you will have 30 seconds to argue the reasons we should collectively deal with a particular item on any of the lists we just went over, or why some items are of little importance. I'll tell you when your 30 seconds are up. You may pass if you wish, but you won't get another turn. There is to be no cross-discussion.

As you read off the items on each list, check to make sure that they are clear to everyone. Point out that these are composite items, reflecting the products of each work group, but that, because they are composites, they may not sound precisely like the originals.

CONDUCT THE ROUND-ROBIN SESSION

Now, let's do some priority setting. We all know what the issues are and how different people feel about them. We will go over each

Note: You may substitute other terms for "most important," for example:

Instructions for Participants

list, item by item, again. You may vote once for the one item that you think is "most important" in each arena (on each list). If there are more than five items on the list, but less than ten, you may have two votes. If there are ten or more, you may have three votes. For example, on this list, there are X items, so you may vote for Y of them.

CONDUCT THE
VOTING SESSION

Great! We've just ranked the items in order of importance (immediacy, order of priority, extent of impact on constituencies, and so on). Clearly, there is consensus on the salience of some items and on the secondary nature of others.

In a moment we will reconvene in our original work groups to turn these issues into operational objectives. But first, let's decide on how many of them we should work on. Should we pick the top three on each list, or all those items that scored X votes or more? Let's pick only our highest priority items. How shall we do it?

**Stage 6: Turning Needs and
Problem Statements into Objectives**

Reconvene in your small groups. Each team will work on the needs and problems statements contributed to the total number agreed to in Stage 8.

Within each group, it will be your job to write performance objec-

Notes to the Convenor

—"requires immediate attention"
—"should be worked on first"
—"most directly affects your constituents"
—"is the most difficult to deal with"

When you have completed one list, go on to the next until all items in each arena have been voted on.

Point out that the salience is considered high where one-third or more of the participants cast a vote for that item.

Let the group decide where the cutoff point should be. Then ask each group's recorder to jot down the priority items decided upon and to designate those that reflected that group's initial contributions (that is, those items that we brought to the interaction group in Stage 4 and that emerged relatively intact on one of the lists used for priority setting in Stage 5).

This is probably the most difficult task for the participants. You can be helpful by suggesting that they use ACTION VERBS (like "conduct," "write," "interview," etc.) as the core of their statements of objectives. This is located at

Instructions for Participants

tives for each of these items. You may attempt to write the performance objectives together with all the members of your group, but you will probably find that it is more effective to divide the responsibility. Some people may prefer to work in pairs or in triplets.

An effective objective should state what the participant would like to be able to do "on the job" after he or she has completed the training program or after other necessary changes in the organization have been completed. You may find yourselves writing more than a single objective in relation to a particular needs or problem item. In writing your objective, follow a procedure you might use in writing a task statement.

> *For example*, in relation to "conducting staff meetings," your objective might be written as follows:
> 1. *Who*: I, the manager of a work unit
> 2. *will do what (behavior)*: will conduct regular (weekly) staff meetings
> 3. *to or with whom*: with all members of my work unit
> 4. *to what end*: for the purpose of (a) communicating information and (b) deciding on work processes and assignments.
> 5. *under whose instructions*: with the approval of my branch manager and the agreement of members of my work unit

Notes to the Convenor

Segment 2 (will do what) of the model shown at the left of this page.

The notes participants wrote on the backs of their original needs and problems cards should be helpful in locating these action verbs.

To prepare yourself adequately, read over the instructions for task analysis in Chapter 3.

Circulate and be available.

Instructions for Participants

Notes to the Convenor

6. *for what purpose or at what level of performance*: such that everyone will have an opportunity to participate and at least two members of the staff will be able to participate at each meeting.

Use a fresh card for each objective.

If you finish before other members in your team, check to see if you can be helpful to one or more of the others in writing their performance objectives.

If your help is not needed, turn your card or cards over and begin listing what you might need to know or what changes would have to be made in the organization in order to do what you have written in the statement of your performance objective. When everyone has completed his statements of objectives, the leader should conduct a meeting of the small group. Those who worked on a particular objective will be given the opportunity to read it aloud.

After the performance objective is read, other members of the group may comment on it. These comments should focus on how clear and well written the statement is. Since this objective is probably not equally important for every member of the group, it is not necessary for everyone to agree on the appropriateness of this objective to his or her own work situation. It is important, however, that the statement of the performance objective is a true

Instructions for Participants   *Notes to the Convenor*

reflection of the collective feelings expressed when choices were made about *needs and problems statements* in the earlier stages of the team planning technique.

It is also important that it be written so as to answer the question:

   1. Who (this may be an individual, group, department, etc.)

   2. will do what (the anticipated behavior)

   3. to or with whom (or for that matter, to or with what)

   4. to what end (the purpose or reason for the behavior)

   5. under whose instructions (or with whose consent, by which rules or regulations, etc.)

   6. at what level of performance (how well or how much)

Once the statement has been refined, it should be written by the group's recorder on a large sheet of paper. While this is happening, the next statement is being read, discussed, refined, and then written.

Stage 7: Working Out the Action Plan
a. *Spelling Out the Centers of Instruction (about 30 minutes)*

This is the final small group (team) activity. Many of the objectives will relate directly to the participant's learning needs. We will focus on these in Stage 7a. We will then focus on actions that must be taken at the organizational level for some of these objectives and

Continue circulating and being available where needed.

Instructions for Participants   *Notes to the Convenor*

for others (which may not require instruction) to be accomplished.

The leader asks members of the group to list all the things that they feel a need to learn in order to be able to perform at the level specified.

In the example given, such a list might include:

- how to organize an agenda
- how to write minutes
- how to make sure everyone has a chance to participate
- how to resolve conflicts

Make the list as concrete as you can, but keep it limited. No more than ten items should be included. Put a star (*) next to the ones the group considers most important. Add these to the large sheet on which the performance objective was written. Attach an additional sheet of paper if needed. In parentheses, add the other items on the list.

Follow the same procedure for each of the statements of performance objectives.

b. Spelling Out Organizational Actions to be taken (about 30 minutes)

Use an identical procedure to spell out those actions that must be taken at the organizational level, and outline some of the objectives that are programmatic rather than educational in nature.

Instructions for Participants

Notes to the Convenor

When you have completed Stage 7 (a and b), select one member of your team to meet with representatives of other teams.

Stage 8: Ratifying the Objectives and Their Order of Priority (about 1 hour)

During a fifteen-minute break and before reconvening in the large group for Stage 8, the representatives of each team should take the sheets of paper on which the statements with performance objectives are written, and post them on the wall in the order of priority or importance. To do this, refer to the ranking of needs and problems statements and the categories under which they fell.

Since these are still on the wall (from Stage 5, priority setting), it should not be difficult to do this. The performance statements, after all, were derived from the needs and problems statements. If the ranking is not clear or if the notes from Stage 5 are ambiguous, arrive at a ranking that represents your collective judgment on what probably reflects the total group's position. Do not worry about being in error. Stage 8 will correct any misperceptions you may have.

Now it is time to reconvene in the large group. As the convenor, I will conduct the meeting. The representatives of the small groups will read the statement written by their own groups, in the order listed (this may require that a particular

The convenor chairs the session as for Stage 5.

Begin by checking to be certain that each of the sheets with performance objectives are properly located (in order of tentative priority). See instructions to participants at left. Make whatever adjustments are needed.

Then conduct the meeting. Give each representative a chance to read the statement(s) he or she put up and to clarify any statement so that it is clearly understood. This is a time for *clarification, not discussion.*

Now ask everyone to give three stars (*) (in their own minds) to those items they feel are most important, and one star to those that are least important. They can put as many items into a three-, two- or one-star category as they wish.

Voting takes place as follows: the convenor points to one statement and asks: "How many gave this item three stars?" The number of hands are multiplied by three. "How many gave it two stars?" The number is multiplied by two. "One star?" All three counts are

Instructions for Participants

representative will read his or her two statements, then wait while others are read, before his or her turn comes up again).

I will then ask the group if this order represents the ranking in terms of importance. It is not necessary that everyone agree on a particular order, but it is important to get a sense of what the group is most interested in.

Notes to the Convenor

added and the total written on top of the sheet. The same is done for all the items on the wall. At the end, they are grouped into three categories. If there were eighteen items to begin with, those six with the highest scores now become three-star items, the next are two-star items, and the last six are one-star items.

You have now completed a very interesting and challenging process. You have not only enabled staff members to spell out their own needs and the problems faced by the organization; you have also helped them see the connections between the organization's problems and their needs. You have taken them a step further, helping them to specify, in performance terms, what needs to be done in order to meet their needs or deal with the organization's problems. Furthermore, you have assisted them in setting an agenda for action. In some cases, the action may require training or staff development activities. In other cases, they may require a shift in management policies and procedures, or agency programs.

NEXT STEPS

If I had never participated in the nominal group process and never conducted an NGT assessment activity, I would want some experience under my belt before attempting the team planning technique. Get some experience with NGT, as described in Activity 4.1. Then try TPT. You will find it easier to handle than a first reading of the instructions might suggest. Modify those instructions so that TPT fits your particular situation.

Consider using it in a context other than that for which it was originally designed. For example, it might be used for decision making with an agency board of directors, with a budget team, or with members of an areawide council on aging. How would you modify the instructions to fit the particular group you have targeted? If the entire process can be completed by a single work group—instead of several teams that interact first independently, then on an interdepartmental basis, and finally on a large group basis—what steps could you eliminate? Are there some other way you might wish to streamline the exercise or expand it to deal with more complex issues? As currently designed, the TPT deals primarily with here-and-now issues. However, the development of performance objectives in Step 6 leads to the development of a "competency" model. Thus, TPT also includes elements of normative assessment. Should the normative aspects be highlighted?

It's your tool and it's in your hands. Experiment. Make it work for you.

SUGGESTED FOR FURTHER READING

Robert F. Bales and F. L. Strodtbeck, "Phases in Group Problem Solving," in M. Alexis and C. Z. Wilson (eds.), *Organizational Decision Making.* Englewood Cliffs, NJ: Prentice-Hall, 1969.

André L. Delbecq, "The Management of Decision Making Within the Firm: Three Strategies for Three Types of Decision Making." *Academy of Management Journal,* 10 December 1967): 329-339.

André L. Delbecq and Andrew H. Van de Ven, "A Group Process Model for Problem Identification and Program Planning," in Neil Gilbert and Harry Specht (eds.), *Planning for Social Welfare: Issues, Models and Tasks.* Englewood Cliffs, NJ: Prentice-Hall, 1977: 333-348.

André L. Delbecq, Andrew H. Van de Ven, and David H. Gustafson, *Group Techniques for Program Planning: A Guide to Nominal and Delphi Processes.* Glenview, IL: Scott Foresman, 1976.

Armand Lauffer, *The Practice of Continuing Education in the Human Services.* New York: McGraw-Hill, 1977: Chapter 12 (Assessment in Continuing Education).

Norman R.F. Maier, *Problem Solving Discussions and Conferences.* New York: McGraw-Hill, 1963: 247-249.

Edward Schoenberger and John Williamson, "Deciding on Priorities and Specific Programs," in Wayne F. Anderson, Bernard J. Frieden, and Michael J. Murphy (eds.), *Managing Human Services.* Washington, DC: International City Management Association, 1977: 162-163.

Phyllis Silverman, *Mutual Help Groups.* Beverly Hills, CA: Sage Publications, 1980.

Andrew H. Van de Ven and André L. Delbecq, "The Effectiveness of Nominal, Delphi, and Interacting Group Decision Making Processes." Unpublished manuscript, no date?

F. H. Veroom, L. D. Grant, and T. J. Cotton, "The Consequences of Social Interaction in Group Problem Solving." *Journal of Applied Psychology,* 53 (August 1969): 338-341.

5. THE DELPHI IS NO ORACLE

ILLUSTRATIONS FROM PRACTICE

Illustration 5.1 Reducing
Task Force Inefficiencies

The associate director of training in a state department of mental health explains:[1]

It didn't seem to make much sense to me to plan statewide training programs in substance abuse without getting some informed opinion on who needed the training most and who should be trained, on the context and format of such training, its location, length, and so on. There were some pretty basic questions—for example, should we focus on psychiatrists and other professionally trained mental health personnel? On lay caregivers? Ex-abusers? Teachers? GPs? Policy and other gatekeepers?

In the past we would convene task forces to help us make policy decisions like these. But I wasn't happy with the work of these task forces. Sometimes the people whose opinion you really want are just not available for the task force. At other times task force members get bogged down in particulars or wind up agreeing on something just to agree. I wasn't ready to give up my use of task forces, but I needed some way to counteract "group think" and to focus task force deliberations. That's where Delphi was so ideal.

1. Illustration 5.1 is reprinted from Armand Lauffer, *The Practice of Continuing Education in the Human Services* (New York: McGraw-Hill, 1977), pp. 166-167.

Before convening regional task forces, I designed an exploratory Delphi questionnaire with eighteen issue statements and sent them to all those people who had agreed to serve, plus a number of others whose opinion I wanted to include. Each issue was stated in policy terms: "Training should be conducted in the home community or on the job rather than at state or regional centers." Or "Users and ex-abusers should be trained to give help to their peers in trouble."

I asked the respondents to rate each item on a five-point scale according to a number of dimensions. For example, I asked them to indicate whether a proposed policy was highly desirable, desirable, neutral, undesirable, or highly undesurable. I then asked them to rate each statement again in accordance with such criteria as estimate of cost, probability of attendance, and feasibility in terms of resources. I left space at the bottom for respondents to add as many as five additional statements, if they wanted to, or to comment on my eighteen.

After summarizing the responses, my staff and I shared the results with each task force. We accounted for regional differences. That way each task force could see how their thinking related to that of other regional planning groups. These preliminary inputs helped to cut down on some of the confusion that usually prevails at first meetings. Based on the first Delphi responses and the discussions reported by my staff at each of the regional meetings, I designed the second Delphi questionnaire.

On those items for which there was a great deal of consensus on desirability and feasibility, no further work was needed. We could just proceed with our planning. But on those items where there were big splits in opinion, or where people thought the idea was good but the feasibility poor, we needed to do a lot of probing. In some cases the clues came from the comments at the bottom of the first questionnaire. We then took what people said during the first task force meeting and put it into our second level of questionnaires. Following several more waves of questionnaires and task force

*meetings, we were able to arrive at some agreement on a
statewide program with considerable variation at the local
levels.*

*There are times when I'm tempted to use Delphi instead of
task forces altogether. I have, in fact, in conference planning.
Delphi is neater; it sharpens opinions and does not degenerate
into group think where the least controversial policy is the
one arrived at, or where some persons sway the rest by the
sheer force of their personalities, status, or just plain
stubbornness. With Delphi, the respondents can stay
anonymous and are more apt to take risks and to be more
honest about their thoughts and feelings.*

DELPHI: WHAT IT IS AND HOW IT IS USED[2]

Delphi is a method of eliciting expert opinion through the use
of successive questionnaires administered to individual panelists,
who are selected on the basis of their perceived expert knowledge
or opinion. They are asked to respond anonymously to a number
of statements, perhaps to evaluate the statements' accuracy,
likelihood, desirability, or cost. Their responses may also include
statements of their own or reasons for their assessment.

The results of individual responses are tabulated and fed back
to all the panelists in a succeeding questionnaire. This feedback
takes the form of a summary of the points of agreement or
disagreement among the experts. Where differences of opinion
are identified, the Delphi design team probes for the reasons for
these differences through a refinement of the statements
presented for panel response.

The Delphi method is generally considered to be fast, inexpensive, and easy to administer. This is not always the case, however,
as respondents who have been participants in a poorly designed

2. Much of this section is abstracted from Armand Lauffer, *Social Planning at the
Community Level* (Englewood Cliffs, NJ: Prentice-Hall, 1978), Chapter 8 (Assessment
Tools), and from Murray Turoff, "The Design of a Policy Delphi," in *Technological
Forecasting and Social Change*, 2 (1970), pp. 149-171. I want to express my appreciation
to Vicki Iucci and Robert Wainess, two former students, for their work in abstracting the
Turoff article.

Delphi process are likely to point out. There are generally two types of Delphi questionnaires: those that attempt to forecast or predict the likelihood that some event or process is likely to occur, and those which are oriented toward an assessment of the best or more feasible policies to take.

Predictive or projective Delphis require the involvement of panelists who are exceptionally knowledgeable about the substantive area being examined. Although their opinions may differ, it is expected that they will nevertheless be well informed. In a policy Delphi, participants are generally those who might be in the best position to evaluate the impact of one or more policies or program priorities. These may include representatives of consumers, providers, or regulatory agencies who are influential in the policymaking process. The policy Delphi is no more intended to arrive at a consensual policy statement than the predictive Delphi aims at forecasting the future. Instead, both aim at achieving clarity even if consensus is impossible. It is therefore crucial that the panelists represent as broad and diverse a group of experts as possible. Also, as indicated previously, respondent anonymity permits a greater degree of risk taking and obviates the possibility of "group think."

The Delphi concept is one of the many by-products of defense industry research. An Air Force-sponsored Rand Corporation study entitled "Project Delphi" was conducted in the early 1950s. It was initially used to estimate the probable effects of a massive nuclear attack on the United States. Later, particularly during the 1960s, the Delphi technique was applied to long-range technological forecasting. Although the method tends to be associated with Norman Dalkey and Olaf Helmer of the Rand Corporation, it has been used extensively in the mid- to late '70s in a variety of human service assessment studies.

In my own practice, I have found Delphi procedures useful in:

- agenda setting for program task forces established by a tricounty area agency on aging

- predicting national trends in the field of mental health and then—with a thirty-member panel of practitioners, government officials, educators, and policymakers—recommending policies for a national strategy of training and continuing education

- identifying neighborhood residents' perceptions of the ideal neighborhood and what they would consider to be an acceptable approximation of that ideal (based on what they and city officials might be willing to put into a redevelopment effort)

- assessing program priorities among various staff groups in a rather complex and highly bureaucratically structured agency, at a time of serious cutbacks that threatened almost 30 percent of the staff and more than half of the agency's services

These might seem at first blush to be rather disparate purposes. But then aren't survey techniques used for many different purposes, or public hearings, or task forces and other interactive groups? Under what conditions, then, might one wish to use a Delphi procedure in assessment? What makes it an especially useful tool in community work and organizational planning? Over the years, I have found the following to be a useful guide in deciding when to use Delphi:

- when adequate information is unavailable and would take too long or be too costly to get

- when the informed opinion of significant parties, including consumers, or potential consumers, may be as important as or more important than hard data

- when the problems at hand or the tasks to be performed are so broad that more individuals are needed to share opinions than can interact in any kind of face-to-face exchange

- when disagreements among individuals are so severe that the communication process must be structured and refereed

- where time is scarce and it would be difficult for the individuals I need to involve to get together for frequent group meetings

- when the heterogeneity and/or anonymity of potential respondents needs to be protected and involving them in interactional groups or even face-to-face exercises like those using nominal group techniques would be dysfunctional

Like the nominal group technique with which it is often compared,[3] Delphi seems ideally suited to structure information gathering and policy exploration in conditions where interaction groups would be counterproductive because of the possible influence of domineering personalities and of participants with greater prestige; the unwillingness of individuals to take a position on an issue or to make their position known before all the "votes" are in; the difficulty and potential danger to a decision-making process of publicly contradicting others; the unwillingness of people to abandon a position once it is taken publicly; or the fear of losing face because an idea may not be grounded in either fact or logic.

PREDICTIVE OR FORECASTING DELPHIS VERSUS POLICY DELPHIS

Put simply, Delphi is a conference on paper with three important features: It collects information in a *quantifiable* manner, it gives *feedback* to those from whom it collected information, it allows respondents to *alter* their responses, and it preserves the *anonymity* of respondents.

The *policy* Delphi has one or more of the following objectives:

- to determine the important issues
- to determine possible policy options on issues
- to determine impact, consequences, and acceptability of options

The *forecasting* Delphi has one or more of these following objectives:

- to determine likely future events
- to predict the likelihood of given future events occurring
- to predict the necessary conditions for a certain event to occur
- to predict likely consequences of the occurrence of a given event

3. See Andrew H. Van de Ven and André L. Delbecq, "The Effectiveness of Nominal, Delphi, and Interacting Group Decision Making Processes." Unpublished manuscript.

All Delphis have four phases:

Phase I. The subject is explored and each individual contributes additional information.

Phase II. The degree of agreement or disagreement in the group is assessed on each point.

Phase III. Underlying reasons for differences are brought out and possibly evaluated.

Phase IV. Previous information is analyzed and fed back for consideration.

These are phases, not steps. A phase may involve more than one step, or more than one phase may be incorporated into a single step. Here is how the steps are taken:

Step 1. Pick a subject. The subject for a policy Delphi should be a policy issue, that is, one for which there are no "correct" solutions but only options that would be supported by some but not by others. Problems of income distribution are clearly policy issues because certain groups benefit under some schemes and different groups benefit under others.

The subject for a forecasting Delphi should be the estimation of future events that have too many variables to be predicted in a certain manner. The predictions of the effects of a nuclear attack on the United States is a classic example of a forecasting Delphi.

Step 2. Pick a respondent group. For the policy Delphi, as diverse a group as possible is desired, in order to explore the widest possible range of options. For a forecasting Delphi, an extremely homogeneous group of experts on the subject is required.

Respondents or panelists should be selected for what each individual can contribute to the group. Each should be knowledgeable on the subject or have opinions that are considered significant. Panelists should be chosen to represent the full range of opinions for a policy Delphi or a wide range of expert knowledge for a forecasting Delphi.

Step 3. Research the subject area. Consider using a brainstorming procedure, face-to-face interviews, a survey of the literature. It is very important in conducting a policy Delphi that you identify all the known options for a given policy issue. If respondents do not have options to comment on, the results are likely to be incomplete.

Step 4. Design and distribute the first-round questionnaire. Sometimes it is called the first "iteration." It includes the first set of predictors or policy options. It must be designed so that responses are given as points on a scale. All answers must be quantifiable, although additional comments by respondents may be encouraged to interpret and support quantitative responses. Room for comments and suggestions and other predictor or policy options should be left on the first-round questionnaire.

Step 5. Design and distribute the second-round questionnaire. This second iteration will look much like the first, with a few notable exceptions. It will begin with feedback, informing respondents of how their responses compared to those of other panelists. Scores, if any, will be included. Second, this iteration should include the comments made by other respondents to justify their positions or to suggest new issues to be addressed. The second-round questionnaire now probes for the reasons responses may have differed in the first iteration.

Rounds go on and on in this manner until scores no longer change. Forecasting Delphis are often completed in three rounds, while policy Delphis may take four, five, or even six rounds to complete.

In the forecasting Delphi, the respondents are "equalized" by being provided relevant baseline information on the present situation. Respondents are then asked to predict the probability or impact of certain future events. Forecasting Delphis are particularly useful when hard facts are not available or when hard data (like those generated in trend studies and in the collection of social and economic indicators) are subject to different interpretations. Respondents are generally selected on the basis of the likelihood that their areas of expertise will complement each other. Diverse expertise is generally sought in order to avoid premature consensus.

In the policy Delphi, the key word is *analysis,* not "prediction" or "decision making." Its main function is to generate the strongest opposing views on potential policy resolutions. If the policy Delphi does act to create consensus, that is all the better, but it does not really have to. The use of a policy Delphi is intended to generate policy *options* and then to explore the impact, consequences, and acceptability of various options. A well-designed policy Delphi will explore and expand dissent, giving different factions a forum for explaining their views.

ACTIVITIES

Activity 5.1:
Examples of Delphi Questionnaires

In the following pages, you will find a series of Delphis used for predictive purposes.[4] Look them over. Try completing them according to the instructions given. Tables 5.5 and 5.6 illustrate one way of summarizing the results in quantitative terms. You will, of course, want to discuss the findings in a more complete manner, once you have designed and conducted your own forecasting Delphi.

TABLE 5.1   Questionnaire #1

This is the first in a series of four questionnaires intended to demonstrate the use of the Delphi Technique in obtaining reasoned opinions from a group of respondents.

Each of the following six questions is concerned with developments in the United States within the next few decades.

In addition to giving your answer to each question, you are also being asked to rank the questions from 1 to 7. Here "1" means that in comparing your own ability to answer this question with what you expect the ability of the other participants to be, you feel that you have the relatively best chance of coming closer to the truth than most of the others, while a "7" means that you regard that chance as relatively least.

---

4. Tables 5.1 through 5.6 are reprinted from Norman C. Dalkey, D. L. Rourke, R. Lewis, and D. Snyder, *Studies in the Quality of Life and Decision Making* (Lexington, MA: Lexington Books, 1972), with permission.

TABLE 5.1   (Continued)

Rank	Question	Answer
☐	1. In your opinion, in what year will the median family income (in 1967 dollars) reach twice its present amount?	☐
☐	2. In what year will the percentage of electric among all automobiles in use reach 50 percent?	☐
☐	3. In what year will the percentage of households reach 50 percent that are equipped with computer consoles tied to a central computer and data bank?	☐
☐	4. By what year will the per-capita amount personal cash transactions (in 1967 dollars) be reduced to one-tenth of what it is now?	☐
☐	5. In what year will power generated by thermonuclear fusion become commercially competitive with hydroelectric power?	☐
☐	6. By what year will it be possible by commercial carriers to get from New York's Times Square to San Francisco's Union Square in half the time that is now required to make that trip?	☐
☐	7. In what year will a man for the first time travel to the Moon, stay for at least one month, and return to Earth?	☐

#*"Never" is also an acceptable answer.*

TABLE 5.1   (Continued)

Please also answer the following question, and give your name (this for identification purposes during the exercise only; no opinions will be attributed to a particular person).

Check One:

☐ I would like   to participate in

☐ I am willing but not anxious   the three remaining

☐ I would prefer not   questionnaries

to participate in
the three remaining
questionnaires

NAME (block letters please)**

##If the respondent is to remain anonymous, you can leave this item out. In order to determine whether all respondents have returned their questionnaires, you may find it helpful to ask them to put their code numbers (for example, the last three digits of their home telephone numbers) on the return envelope and have your secretary "log in" the returns as they arrive. That way it becomes possible to followup on no-returns.—AL

TABLE 5.2 Questionnaire #2

This is the second in our series of four Delphi questionnaires.

The same seven questions that had been posed in the first questionnaire are repeated below, together with information on the median and the interquartile range (IQR) of the first-round responses. (The IQR is the interval containing the middle 50 percent of the responses.) Please reconsider your previous estimate and change it if you wish. Whenever your present answer is outside the IQR, briefly state your reason why you think the answer should be a year that much earlier (or later) than that given by the majority of respondents. (No such reason needs to be given when your answer is inside the IQR.)

Question	Median	IQR	Your Old Answer	Your New Answer	Reason Your Answer Is Below or Above the IQR
1. In your opinion, in what year will the median family income (in 1967 dollars) reach twice its present amount?	85	80-92	F I		
2. In what year will the percentage of electric among all automobiles in use reach 50 percent?	90	85-2012	L L E		
3. In what year will the percentage of households reach 50 percent that are equipped with computer consoles tied to a central computer and data bank?	2000	90-2075	D I		
4. By what year will the per-capita amount of personal cash transactions (in 1967 dollars) be reduced to one-tenth of what it is now?	90	82-2000	N B Y		
5. In what year will power generated by thermonuclear fusion become commercially competitive with hydroelectric power?	90	79-2005	D R.		
6. By what year will it be possible by commercial carriers to get from New York's Times Square to San Francisco's Union Square in half the time that is now required to make that trip?	80	75-85	H E L M		
7. In what year will a person for the first time travel to the Moon, stay for at least one month, and return to Earth?	77½	75-85	E R		

NAME: ....

TABLE 5.3 Questionnaire #3

The same familiar seven questions are restated below, together with the median and interquartile ranges (IQRs) or the twenty-three second-round responses. Also included are some brief arguments as to why the estimates should be either earlier or later than those within the IQR.

Please reconsider your previous estimates (which are attached), and revise them if you wish, giving the stated reasons for raising or lowering them the weight you think they deserve. (If there is no change in your previous response, please reinsert it under "your new answer.")

If your present answer lies outside the indicated IQR, briefly state in the last column why you think the argument that had been given in favor of an estimate on the opposite side of the IQR from your own is unacceptable. (In other words, if your estimate is high, refute the argument for a low estimate; if your estimate is low, refute the argument for a high estimate.)

Question	Median	IQR	Argument in Favor of an Earlier Date	Argument in Favor of a Later Date	Your New Answer	Your Critique of Arguments Unacceptable to You
1. In your opinion, in what year will the median family income (in 1967 dollars) reach twice its present amount?	1985	1980-1990	There is a 10 percent annual inflation.	The GNP goes up only 4 percent per year.		
			Union demands will bring this about sooner, through amendments to the "guideposts."	There will be a decrease in the number of hours worked per family.		
			The number of workers per family will rise.	Increasing inflation will devaluate the dollar.		
			Income will grow faster than GNP as wage earners take a greater share of productivity earnings due to new technology.	A major business depression may be expected.		
				Real family income rose only 50 percent in the last twenty-five years.		
				The productivity per family will not grow so fast because neither the size of the family unit nor productivity per family will.		

(Continued)

TABLE 5.3 (Continued)

2. In what year will the percentage of electrical among all automobiles in use reach 50 percent?	1995	1985-2020	The first use will be for local travel, which will rapidly exceed 50 percent, in view of urban development.
			Developments in nuclear-power cost/effectiveness and energy storage point to an earlier date.
			Pollution will force improvements in the combustion engine.
			Batteries don't provide enough power or range.
			Battery recharging is too inconvenient.
			The oil industry will resist this.
			Electric cars will be too expensive.
			Natural-gas fueled turbines have a better chance.
			There are enormous problems in economic conversion to electric energy in small packages, hence delay until fossil fuels exhausted.
3. In what year will the percentage of households reach 50 percent that are equipped with computer consoles tied to a central computer and data bank?	2010	1985-2100	The technology is here now. This will be combined with your telephone.
			Computers are getting cheaper fast.
			We need to reduce the volume of mail.
			Progress in computerization in commercial and social organization will require individual computers in homes; fifteen years should do it (analogy: TV in 1945-60).
			The social demand will not be great enough, considering the high cost.
			The main use would be for education and reference; we are several generations away from the intellectual level that can use such teachers and librarians.
			Cost-effectiveness of personal data banks and decentralized computers will rise, and they are preferable because of privacy.
			Who needs instant bank statements that badly?

TABLE 5.3 (Continued)

Question	Median	IQR	Argument in Favor of an Earlier Date	Argument in Favor of a Later Date	Your New Answer	Your Critique of Arguments Unacceptable to You
4. By what year will the per-capita amount of personal cash transactions (in 1967 dollars) be reduced to one-tenth of what it is now?	1985	1985-1990	Everyone will soon be assigned a combination credit card and social security card. Studies by the banking industry are already under way to computerize monetary transactions. Connecticut already has a statewide credit card.	We seem to be already approaching the minimum now, and therefore may never reach that low a level in the near future.		
5. In what year will power generated by thermonuclear fusion become commercially competitive with hydroelectric power?	1985	1977-2025	Water shortage within 10 years will force this development. Power demands, especially in connection with desalination, will rapidly become so great that thermonuclear power production will be generally accepted. Decentralization of population centers and cost of distribution favor nuclear power. The next drought will be worldwide.	Fission-generated power is not yet commercially competitive; fusion-generated power will require development of basic technology, with immense problems to overcome. There is little economic incentive since electric power is cheap. Tidal power is yet untapped. The cost of hydroelectric facilities is shared, there is no fuel cost, and maintenance is lower. Efficient containment of thermonuclear energy seems to be completely out of the question.		

(Continued)

TABLE 5.3 (Continued)

6. By what year will it be possible by commercial carriers to get from New York's Time Square to San Francisco's Union Square in half the time that is now required to make that trip?	1976	1975-1980	Rapid-transit approaches to the airports will be set up. Baggage will be handled faster. The Concorde will appear on U.S. schedules by 1973, and a U.S. SST by 1975.	Supersonic flight is not possible over land barriers. Now it takes 15 m + 4h 30m + 30m = 5h 15m; with SST it would take 10m + 2h 15m + 20m = 2h 45m, which is more than 50 percent. Increase in aircraft speed alone will not achieve this so soon; other developments (vertical takeoff, etc.) will be required, which will take somewhat longer.
7. In what year will a person for the first time travel to the Moon, stay for at least one month, and return to Earth?	1977	1975-1980	After a first successful landing, only about three years will be required to develop life-cycle equipment for an extended stay. The capability will exist in the early 1970s; national prestige and curiosity will dictate the decision. Mission profiles compatible with Apollo/LEM hardware/ payload capabilities will be available in the early 1970s.	Regular Moon trips will not occur until 1980, and a Moon station not until after 1990. The rise in cost will force a slowdown in the Moon program, especially in view of alternative goals (e.g., oceanographic research).

TABLE 5.4 Questionnaire #4

This is the last in our series of four questionnaires. Together with each of the seven questions, restated once more below, you are given the third-round median and IQR of the 23 responses received, as well as a summary of statements critical of the reasons that had been given in response to the second questionnaire.

Please reconsider (and possibly revise) your previous estimates once more in the light of the arguments (see attached Questionnaire 3) and counterarguments that had been advanced for and against raising or lowering them.

Question	Median	IQR	Counterarguments in Defense of an Earlier Date	Counterarguments in Defense of a Later Date	Your Final Answer
1. In your opinion, in what year will the median family income (in 1967 dollars) reach twice its present amount?	1985	1980-1990	The GNP rose 4.3 percent before the "guideposts" were removed; now it will go up faster.	Even if income grows faster than 4 percent rate of GNP, it will not double in twenty or thirty years.	
			Advanced skills will sharply increase income.	Greater productivity of direct labor is largely offset by indirect labor due to maintenance, etc. of more sophisticated equipment.	
			A major depression (as opposed to a healthy recession) is very unlikely under current and future federal safeguards.	The inflation argument is beside the point since the question is phrased in terms of 1967 dollars.	
			Family size is not of critical importance; husband and wife are the essential income producers.	The union bargaining position has been weakened by strikes; federal intervention is more likely to be demanded in future.	
				The number of workers per family will not rise, because as income increases, families tend to subdivide into new units.	

(Continued)

TABLE 5.4 (Continued)

2. In what year will the percentage of electrical among all automobiles in use reach 50 percent?	1995	1985-2011	The later-date arguments overlook the political pressure Battery and fuel cell improvements will, in the 1970s, provide sufficient power and range (cf., e.g., Ayres's envelope curves). Inconvenience will be minimized because recharging can be automatic upon garaging. Resistance of the oil industry can be countered by positive response of electric utilities. The later-date proponents seem to overlook the possibility of the car to tie into a power grid.	If it were not for pollution, this would occur even later than 2000. Energy storage would have to improve by ten orders of magnitude. Consumers buy cars for long-distance high-speed driving.
4. By what year will the per-capita amount of personal cash transactions (in 1967 dollars) be reduced to one-tenth of what it is now?	1985	1985-1990	The statement about our approaching a minimum now is not based on fact.	Credit will not be extended so generally, i.e., not until bank accounts and payrolls are tied into the system, and this will take more time. "Studies" do not mean immediate implementation. Only 5 percent of my present expenditures are in cash; this would be hard to reduce to one-tenth. The greatest portion of personal cash transactions today is in the lower-income groups, and the impact of the earlier-date arguments on them will be minimal.

TABLE 5.4 (Continued)

Question	Median	IQR	Counterarguments in Defense of an Earlier Date	Counterarguments in Defense of a Later Date	Your Final Answer
5. In what year will power generated by thermonuclear fusion become commercially competitive with hydroelectric power?	1985	1980–2030	Pressures regarding this on government and industry will escalate exponentially. The "out of the question" statement is of the form "airplanes will never fly."	Technical feasibility of plasma containment is not demonstrated or in sight. The earlier-date argument merely supports the case for fission-generated power—which may be the real competitor, rather than hydroelectric power. The drought argument is too speculative for comment.	
6. By what year will it be possible by commercial carriers to get from New York's Time Square to San Francisco's Union Square in half the time that is now required to make that trip?	1976	1975–1980	The airlines have identified ground transportation and "people handling" as their top-priority assignment. Many downtown rooftop airports will be built for fast local air transport. Supersonic flights take place daily over the southwestern United States.	High-speed land transportation will take longer to develop. The rapid-transit argument is not good enough, not until we have something faster than the SST under development. Rapid ground transit already exists; increased air traffic will further increase time on the ground.	
7. In what year will a person for the first time travel to the Moon, stay for at least one month, and return to Earth?	1977	1975–1980	We are still competing with the Russians. Regular Moon trips will occur in the early 1970s; a Moon station is not required for a month's stay. "Regular Moon trips" was not part of the question.	The argument for an earlier date is excessively optimistic as to resources to be devoted to this project by the United States or Russia. Reliability demands will cause delay.	

TABLE 5.5   Summary of Outcome

	IQR	Median	"Expert"* Median
1. Family income doubled	1982-90	1985	1985
2. Electric autos 50 percent	1985-2000	1995	1997
3. Home computer consoles	1985-2075	2010	1985
4. Credit card economy	1985-90	1985	1987½
5. Economical fusion power	1985-2030	1990	1987½
6. N.Y. to S.F. in ½ time	1975-80	1976	1975
7. Man on moon one month	1975-80	1977	1975½

*Median of the eight individuals who ranked themselves highest. The cutoff point was usually two or three.

TABLE 5.6 Convergence of Range with Successive Questionnaires

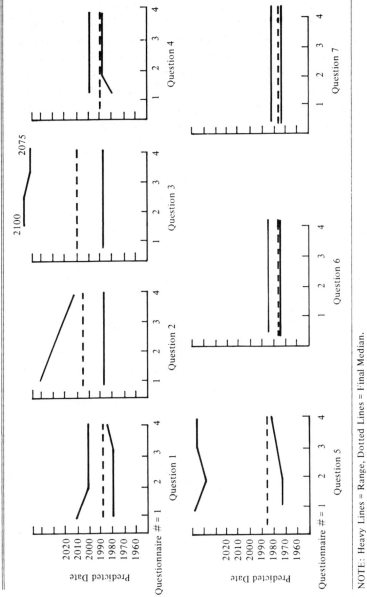

NOTE.: Heavy Lines = Range, Dotted Lines = Final Median.

111

Activity 5.2:
Designing Your Own Delphi

It is also possible to design a Delphi questionnaire that includes both predictive and judgmental or policy considerations. Several years ago, Charles Garvin from the University of Michigan and I conducted the study of mental health education mentioned earlier in this chapter. On the next page, you will find Section F of our first-wave questionnaire. Notice that it uses several codes. In our instructions to the respondents (Item B), we provided them with a code sheet that instructed them on how to enter their responses in a uniform manner.

Item B: Code Sheet

A. *Probability* (How likely is this change to occur within the next ten years?)

Codes

1. Very probable—almost certain to happen
2. Probable—indications of this happening
3. Either way—this might or might not happen
4. Improbable—indications that this won't happen
5. Very Improbable—almost certain not to happen

B. *Importance to Mental Health Services* (consumers, problems, practices)

Codes

1. Very Important—crucial impact on major services
2. Important—significant impact on services
3. Slightly important—little impact on services
4. Unimportant—no impact on services

C. *Desirability* (How desirable do you feel that the impact of this change will be on the mental health field?)

Codes

1. Very desirable—very beneficial
2. Desirable—beneficial
3. Undesirable—harmful
4. Very undesirable—very harmful

D. *Service Provider Code*

P:MD	Psychiatrist (M.D.)
PSY	Psychologist
SW	Social worker
N	Nurse
T	Teacher
ALT	Person trained in alternative institution, i.e., individual regardless of previous training who is trained by such institutions as a street clinic or therapeutic commune
PER	Peer (another individual usually from the culture of the individual)
O	No one; approach will be obsolete
Para-1	Paraprofessional with little education
Para-2	Paraprofessional with some college education but no professional education
F-F	Family members and friends

Section F

The following is a list of therapeutic approaches used in the mental health field. Please indicate whether you think the uses of such methods will have increased or decreased by the year 1984, whether that is a desirable state, and what type(s) of service providers will be using the method.

Method	Increase–I Decrease–D Stay Same–S	Desirable Code C	Types of Service Providers Code E: May Use More Than One
1. Insight-oriented, psychoanalytic, or other "uncovering" therapies; ego-psychological approaches			
2. Rational approaches, logical reasoning (reality therapy, rational-emotive therapy)			
3. Behavior modification, systematic desensitization			
4. Transactional analysis			
5. Approaches leading to greater awareness (e.g., Gestalt)			
6. Approaches using linkages between physical and emotional states, e.g., rolfing, biofeedback, massage			
8. Approaches enhancing interpersonal sensitivities and communications (e.g., encounter, sensitivity training, growth experiences in groups)			
9. Therapeutic communities, residential settings			
10. Mechanical, electrical and chemical means of behavior control			
11. Peer approaches (e.g., "reevaluation counselling," "support groups")			
12. Please add any others you think important			

Activity 5.2:
Designing Your Own Policy Delphi Questionnaire

Now it is your turn to design a policy Delphi questionnaire. Review the phases and steps discussed in the previous pages and look over the range of rating or evaluative "descriptors" found in Table 5.7. I have borrowed them from the Turoff article discussed earlier. They are fairly standard for any policy Delphi questionnaire.

TABLE 5.7   Evaluative Descriptors

Importance, Priority, or Relevance

Very Important	• a most relevant point
	• first-order priority
	• has direct bearing on major issues
	• must be resolved, dealt with or treated
Important	• is relevant to the issue
	• second-order priority
	• significant impact but not until other items are treated
	• does not have to be fully resolved
Slightly Important	• insignificantly relevant
	• third-order priority
	• has little importance
	• not a determining factor to major issue
Unimportant	• no priority
	• no relevance
	• no measurable effect
	• should be dropped as an item to consider

(Continued)

TABLE 5.7   (Continued)

Feasibility

Definitely Feasible
- no hindrance to implementation
- no R&D required
- no political roadblocks
- acceptable to the public

Possibly Feasible
- some indication this is implementable
- some R&D required
- no political roadblocks
- acceptable to the public

Possibly Infeasible
- some indication this is unworkable
- significant unanswered questions

Definitely Infeasible
- all indications are negative
- unworkable
- cannot be implemented

Confidence (in validity of argument or premise)

Certain
- low risk of being wrong
- decision based upon this will not be wrong because of this "fact"
- most inferences drawn from this will be true

Reliable
- some risk of being wrong
- willing to make a decision based on this but recognizing some chance of error
- some incorrect inferences can be drawn

Risky
- substantial risk of being wrong
- not willing to make a decision based on this alone
- many incorrect inferences can be drawn

Unreliable
- great risk of being wrong
- of no use as a decision basis

TABLE 5.7 (Continued)

Desirability (effectiveness or benefits)

Very Desirable
- will have a positive effect and little or no negative effect
- extremely beneficial
- justifiable on its own merit

Desirable
- will have a positive effect; negative effects minor
- beneficial
- justifiable as a by-product or in conjunction with other items

Undesirable
- will have a negative effect
- harmful
- may be justified only as a by-product of a very desirable item, not justified as a by-product of a desirable item

Very Undesirable
- will have a major negative effect
- extremely harmful
- not justifiable

Probability (likelihood)

Very Probable
- almost certain to occur
- strong indications of this happening

Probable
- better than a fifty-fifty chance of occurring
- some indications of this happening

Either Way
- fifty-fifty
- could go either way

Improbable
- less than a fifty-fifty chance of occurring
- some indications of this not happening

Very Improbable
- almost certain not to occur
- strong indications against this happening

For your first practice effort, draw up five policy statements or program recommendations that have implications for your agency or for a particular consumer population with which you are concerned. Use at least two descriptors for respondents to use in rating the policies or programs. Use the blank form found on the next page. Duplicate sufficient copies of the form for testing with a group of colleagues or friends. Get their reactions to its utility in the current form and make some changes. Based on their feedback, how would you design your second-wave questionnaire? The following are two examples:

(1) To make up the slack in personnel resources due to recent funding cutbacks, the agency should develop a cadre of volunteers to work with and under the direction of agency caseworkers.

Desirability				*Feasibility*			
Hi		*Lo*		Hi			Lo
1	*2*	*3*	*4*	1	2	3	4

(2) The growing numbers of handicapped persons requiring services aimed at increasing their independence will become a major concern of the agency during the next two years.

Importance				*Confidence*			
Hi		Lo		Hi			Lo
1	2	3	4	1	2	3	4

Policy Delphi statements are essentially normative assessments. They focus on what "ought to be." In example 1, the "agency *should*." In the second example, "services . . . will become a major concern" can be viewed as both a predictive and a normative statement. The evaluative descriptors "desirability and feasibility" or "importance and confidence" are the tipoffs. Delphi questionnaires can be all predictive, all normative, or all descriptive (to assess current perceptions and points of view). They can also be all three. It is important in your design to be certain of whether you are examining what is, what is likely to be, or what ought to be. A worksheet for policy Delphi statements appears on page 119.

Policy Statements		Hi 4 3	Lo 2 1		Hi 4 3	Lo 2 1	

SUGGESTIONS FOR FURTHER READING

Norman C. Dalkey and Olaf Helmer, "An Experimental Application of the Delphi Process to the Use of Experts." *Management Sciences,* 9 (1963).

Norman C. Dalkey, D. L. Rourke, R. Lewis, and D. Snyder, *Studies in the Quality of Life: Delphi and Decision-Making.* Lexington, MA: Lexington Books, 1972.

André L. Delbecq, Andrew H. Van de Ven, and David H. Gustafson, *Group Techniques for Program Planning: A Guide to Nominal Group and Delphi Processes.* Glenview, IL: Scott, Foresman, 1976.

Olaf Halmer, "Convergence of Expert Consensus Through Feedback,"*Rand Paper*-2973. Santa Monica, CA: Rand Corporation, 1964.

Armand Lauffer, *The Practice of Continuing Education in the Human Services.* New York: McGraw-Hill, 1977.

Armand Lauffer, *Social Planning at the Community Level.* Englewood Cliffs, NJ: Prentice-Hall, 1978: Chapter 8.

Harold Linstone and Murray Turoff, *The Delphi Method: Techniques and Applications,* Reading, MA: Addison-Wesley, 1975.

Murray Turoff, "The Design of a Policy Delphi." *Technological Forecasting and Social Change,* 2 (1970): 140-171.

Harold Sackman, *Delphi Critique.* Lexington, MA: Lexington Books and the Rand Corporation, 1975.

6. MAY THE FORCE BE WITH YOU
Using Force Field Analysis

ILLUSTRATIONS FROM PRACTICE

Illustration 6.1: The Empire Strikes Back[1]

As a supervisor in a group home for boys, I've got my share of management problems. Things seemed to turn around after I'd taken the guys out to see The Empire Strikes Back. *For a while everybody was into flowing with the force. There seemed to be a good feeling between the kids and between them and me. One of the guys I had had most trouble with even said, "May the force be with you" to me just before he went to bed. I decided to make "the force" work for them too.*

One of the problems I have with the group is that I don't want them to reject ideas because they come from me, and I also don't want them to accept my suggestions because they're being made by an adult in an authority position. As far as I'm concerned, I want them to become more open and active in criticizing what they see as helpful suggestions from adults and in seeking feedback from adults on their own ideas about how they should handle behavior or programming issues.

So I decided to chart out the forces at play here, using a force field diagram. Taking a blank sheet of paper, I drew a line down the middle. On the left side, I jotted down the forces for achieving this kind of open interdependence. On the right side, I jotted down all the forces against achieving that

---

1. Illustration 6.1 inspired by a training package designed by Charles C. Jung, formerly of the Center for Research on Utilization of Scientific Knowledge at the Institute for Social Research of the University of Michigan.

objective. The line in the middle represented where I figured things were right now. And it was right in the middle of the page because the forces pushing for achievement of my goal were counterbalanced by the forces against it. Here's what my first attempt at diagramming what these forces looked like.

Force Field 1: Interdependence Between the Group and Me

Forces for Interdependence opposite of goal	Forces against Interdependence goal
Kids want to try their ideas.	Kids afraid their ideas will look poor to others.
Kids want good ideas from adults.	Kids used to letting adults tell them what to do.
I want kids to question my suggestions, but not just accept or reject them.	Kids afraid to criticize me or other adults openly.
	I am frequently judgmental in my criticism.

I wasn't particularly happy with this diagram because I knew something was missing from it. I decided to ask the kids themselves the next time we had a house meeting. I told them I was having trouble "going with the force"; maybe they were too. I shared some examples of the kind of issues I was concerned about and asked them for their reactions. Well, I got 'em. Around one of the issues, figuring out a better way of sharing household responsibilities, there was a lot of silence and hasty glances between the boys. Around another issue, dealing with some of the neighborhood complaints about noisiness at nights, everybody participated. The boys reacted to my ideas and shared a lot of their own.

I learned two things from our discussion. The first is that an additional "force for" was actively to ask the kids for their reactions. A "force against" was that there seemed to be a negative norm about talking to adults about certain kinds of issues—particularly when it meant "ratting" on somebody else or apple polishing. Clearly, the kids in a leadership position in the group were the ones who could determine who would talk about what issue and who wouldn't. Like on the noise issue, Phil and Evans talked up. On the housekeeping issue I could see Phil glancing around the room and everyone checking on what was on his mind. Nobody said anything.

Well, I was now ready to add to my force field. I put a number one by that force that I thought would yield most movement toward my goal, if that force could be changed. Then I put a two by the force that I thought would result in the second greatest amount of movement, and so on. The second thing I did was to rate each force in terms of how hard or easy I thought it might be to make some change in it. It occurred to me that maybe some of the forces I'd listed weren't really forces at all. So I went back and rated each one again on the basis of how clear I was about whether it really was a significant force. Here's what my second stab looked like.

Force Field 2: Interdependence Between the Group and Me

Forces for Interdependence opposite of goal	Forces against Interdependence goal
(clear) (3) (easy) Kids want to try their ideas.	(medium) (10) (unclear) Kids afraid their ideas will look poor to others.
(partly clear) (6) (medium) Kids want good ideas from adults.	(easy) (9) (clear) Kids used to letting adults tell them what to do.
(partly clear) (7) (easy) I want kids to question and criticize	(medium) (8) (partly clear) Kids afraid to criticize me or other adults openly.
(partly clear) (4) (medium) I actively ask for kids to get involved and to make suggestions.	(hard) (5) (partly clear) I am frequently judgmental in my criticism.
	(hard) (1) (partly clear) Kids have norm of not talking.
	(medium) (2) (unclear) Peer leaders support norm of not talking with adults on some issues.

Now all this may seem like a "Mickey Mouse" way of doing things. When I looked over my diagram, it all seemed so obvious. But to tell you the truth, it wasn't all that obvious until I started mapping things out on paper. Sometimes you know in your gut that something is wrong or that it ought to be moving in some other direction. When you have a feeling that you're flowing with the forces or against them, or for that matter that the forces are actively working against each other in directions that aren't very helpful, it's good to sit down by yourself and to chart things out. It helps you understand where it is you want to go and what you have to do to get there.

USING FORCE FIELD ANALYSIS

It is my impression that the group home supervisor made adequate use of force field analysis. But he missed the boat on at least two counts. First, he could have involved the boys actively in sketching the force field itself. By drawing on their knowledge and modeling precisely the kind of behavior he was aiming for, he might have done a better job of assessment while at the same time using assessment as an energizing process. Second, by not being more specific about the desired objective or about the specific actors in the situation who might impact on the forces acting on the achievement of that objective, his analysis was only partially complete and partially useful. He could have done better.

In the pages that follow, we will explore a variety of situations that are amenable to a force field analysis and we will walk through each of the steps required to perform the analysis adequately. First, a few words about the technique itself.

The use of force field analysis (FFA) derives from the work of Kurt Lewin. Lewin's psychoecological model perceived the individual, or for that matter any other organism, as existing within a life or organization space. He called this a "field." It could be schematically diagrammed at any particular point in time. The life or organizational space is composed of all those factors which might influence the behavior of the organism examined.[2] Forces might be exerted on that organism by norms,

2. Refer to Chapter 2, in which we used mapping exercises to explore the ecological relationships between individuals or organizations and their environments.

economic pressures, changes in physical surroundings, expressed needs of others, and so on.

Within the environment there are *driving* forces that induce the organism toward some new direction or change. There are also *restraining* forces that either tend to reinforce the status quo or support the organism's resistance to change. When the driving and restraining forces are of roughly the same magnitude, we tend to experience a steady state. In Lewin's terms, this is a "dynamic equilibrium," one that is always subject to change in one direction or another.

Over the past two decades, practitioners have found FFA useful in analyzing the forces that might be activated to promote a desired change in an individual, family group, organization, larger community, and, indeed, a larger society.

Arthur Kuriloff found FFA to be an extremely useful tool for diagnosing work-related problems in organizations and discovering alternatives that might be available for impacting on those problems.[3] He describes a situation in which a group of professionals working on a government contract developed "a habit of drifting in late from lunch," whereas under the terms of the contract they were required to punch time clocks for governmental accounting purposes. On investigation, their tardy behavior was found to stem, in part, from their resentment at being treated like hourly workers, contrary to their perceptions of their professional status. A second restraining force, perhaps of lesser magnitude, was their dislike for rushing the noon meal, for which only thirty minutes were allotted by company policy. Furthermore, many of the staff ate in the company's cafeteria, which tended to be overcrowded and slow during the noon hour. Thus, ecological factors also impinged on individual behavior. Figure 6.1 shows these forces schematically.

The primary driving forces were identified as pressure from management, which in itself reflected pressure from the government agency to have staff return to work on time. A second force was the group norm that established twenty minutes as a reasonable limit for tardiness. Lateness beyond that point was considered unacceptable by most of the engineers.

3. Arthur H. Kuriloff, *Organizational Development for Survival* (Washington, DC: American Management Association, 1972), pp. 132-136.

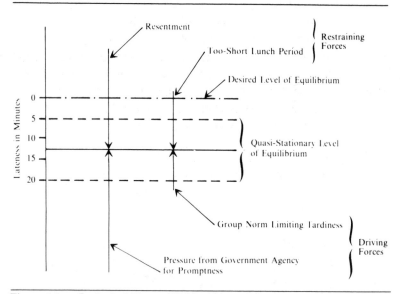

Figure 6.1   Ecological Factors Impinging on Behavior

A practitioner trying to make changes in the situation might use one of the following alternatives: (1) increasing one or both driving forces, (2) reducing the restraining forces, or (3) a combination of the two approaches. Organizational analysts have found that it is often more productive to reduce restraining forces than to increase driving forces, the latter often increasing tension and inflaming resistance. One way to start, therefore, might be to unfreeze the situation by reducing the restraining forces. Once the situation has been unfrozen, an increase in the driving forces might be set in motion.

The existing pattern having been unfrozen and new behaviors set into motion, the situation will have to be stabilized or "refrozen" at a new level. Frequently, the practitioner will find that establishment of a new behavioral pattern can best be achieved through involving members of the group or others who can impact on the particular forces identified. But who are these critical actors? What might be the level of their involvement? There are times when forces (such as national economic conditions that may affect a particular problem situation) are totally outside of the control of the actors being affected by that situation. Trying to reduce such restraining or driving forces would seem to be a waste of time. Selecting another force that may be more amenable to change would seem to be the wiser choice. This focus on critical actors, and an examination of those forces that are amenable to change, are major features in the use of FFA by Brager and Holloway.[4] Their concerns are aimed at improving the ways human service organizations function and determining alternative action strategies for influencing change at the community level. The steps outlined below are drawn from their work.

STEPS IN THE FORCE FIELD ANALYSIS PROCESS

Once you have defined the problem situation or assessed a need and made a preliminary decision about a change goal, you are ready to use force field analysis. Unlike some of the other tools discussed in this book, FFA is used to assess the forces in the ecological environment that contribute to a problem or that can be activated objectives. Some of these may be dismissed out of hand as impractical or out of synch with the agency's perception of its mandate. Usually, however, there are a range of objectives and actions that have varying potential for solving a particular problem, any of which may be acceptable to the critical actors in an organization. FFA can be used at any point in the process of goal development to explore the feasibility or acceptability of the goal, or to choose from among alternative action possibilities.

Before you try your hand at doing a force field analysis, let's review some of the terminology we will be using. On the following pages, I have defined the key terms with which you will need to be familiar.[5]

If, on reading the definitions, some may seem a bit unclear, do not worry about it. Once you begin doing the exercise, you will find yourself defining actors and forces according to the glossary. You may need to refer back to the glossary at any point at which

4. George Brager and Stephen Holloway, *Changing Human Service Organizations* (New York: Free Press, 1978), pp. 107-128.

5. I am thankful to Gerald Matthews, a former student, for generating these definitions from the literature. He draws in particular from the Brager and Holloway book referred to in note 4.

you may have to make a judgment. Having looked over the glossary, you are now ready to do your own force field analysis.

Think of a situation that requires intervention on your part. It can be in your professional or your personal life. For example, you may wish to alter some of your relationships with friends or members of your family, or you may wish to have clients do the same. The problem you choose to deal with may revolve around potential political action at the neighborhood level, or the situation may stem from job dissatisfaction and a growing burnout syndrome at the agency. Once you have decided what you want to work on, follow the instructions for Activity 6.1. Use the force field balance sheet that follows. If you find the space allowed too limiting, draw up your own balance sheet on a piece of 8½ × 11 paper. Better still, if you choose to do a force field analysis with others, use a piece of newsprint or the chalkboard. I would think, however, that before you try using force field analysis with others, you would want greater familiarity with the steps and procedures.

GLOSSARY OF TERMS USED IN FORCE FIELD ANALYSIS

Actors

Critical actors. Individuals or groups that must support a change effort or maintenance of the status quo in order for it to become or remain a reality. Critical actors may include funders, administrators, parents, informal leaders in a peer group, or any of a number of resource gatekeepers.

Facilitating actors. These are of two types: (1) those whose approval must be obtained before matters can be brought to the attention of critical actors; and (2) those whose approval, disapproval, or neutrality may have a decisive impact on critical actors. In effect, these are the gatekeepers to access to the critical actors. Distinguishing between the two categories can be helpful in design of a change strategy.

Forces

Driving forces. Those forces that, when increased, alter behavior of those affected in some desired or planned manner.

Redundant forces. Those forces that either are not amenable to change or over which none of the critical actors has any control. Can be either driving or restraining forces.

Restraining forces. Those forces that, when increased, reinforce the status quo or lead to continuation of a condition that is the antithesis of the change goal.

Unpredictable forces. Either (1) those forces that have been designated as "uncertain" in amenability to change, potency, or consistency; or (2) those forces that are rated "low" on consistency.

Working forces. Those forces that are judged to be moderate to be high on amenability to influence, potency, and consistency. These are the principle forces to be modified or acted upon in a planned change effort. The greater the number of working forces on both sides of the force field balance sheet, the greater the likelihood of successful intervention.

Amenability, Consistency, and Potency

Amenability to change or influence. Refers to a force's potential for modification (such as being decreased, if a restraining force, or increased, if a driving force).

Consistency. The extent to which a force is expected to remain stable over time, unless intervention efforts or the consequences of other actions and events are likely to create a change in its presence or potency.

Potency. The actual or potential impact of a force on maintaining the status quo, resisting change, or achieving the change goal; that is, the force's potential strength, the extent of its influence.

All three of the above can be estimated in terms of three measures: high, low, or uncertain.

ACTIVITY 6.1:
DOING A FORCE FIELD ANALYSIS

Using the force field balance sheet, that follows, complete the following steps.

Step 1. Describe the problem or need in succinct terms. This is the situation you want changed. Fill in the appropriate box.

Step 2. Specify the goal or objective to be reached. Be as operationally specific as possible (for example, "lunchtime tardiness will be eliminated," "cutbacks will take place without limiting agency effectiveness," "family members will agree that they are each involved in decision-making according to the rules agreed to in the counseling session"). Which of these are specific enough to be measured?

Step 3. Now identify all the *restraining* forces: those that contribute to the problem or that mitigate against amelioration or goal achievement.

Step 4. List the *driving* forces: those that currently or potentially move in the direction of the change goal.

Step 5. Estimate the *potency, consistency,* and *amenability to change* of each of the forces listed. Do this by designating each as H (high), L (low), or U (uncertain) in the appropriate column to the left of the restraining forces and to the right of the driving forces.

Step 6. Having indicated which ones you feel are amenable to manipulation, identify the actors who you feel are best able to influence those forces. Jot down their names in the box below the list of forces. Then indicate which actor is most likely to be influential as regards the forces identified. For example, if the "executive director" is listed on line A and your assessment is that he is most likely to influence restraining forces 2 and 3 and driving force 4, put the letter A in the column closest to the driving (near right) or restraining (near left) forces. Line X stands for you, your staff, your group, or whomever is completing the form and is committed to the change goal. Some people might end the process at this point. I have found it useful to take an additional step before trying to map out an action strategy aimed at achieving my goal or objective.

Step 7. Identify those forces you consider to be *working* forces, because they are high (H) on potency, consistency, and amenability to change. Circle the number to the left or to the right of those forces (depending on whether they are restraining or driving forces). Write a W in the margin. Now identify those forces you consider uncertain (U) on amenability, potency, and consistency, or which is low (L) on consistency. These are the *Unpredictable* forces. They represent uncertainty. To designate them on your balance sheet, draw a question mark (?) in the margin to the right or left. Finally, there is one last ministep in the assessment process. Identify those forces that are low (L) on amenability or for which you could find no influential actors. These are *Redundant* from your point of view, because no one seems to be able to do anything about them. Cross out the number to the right or left, and put a large O in the appropriate margin.

AFTER THE FORCE FIELD
BALANCE SHEET, WHAT NEXT?

Having completed the FFA balance sheet and having assessed each force's amenability to change, potency, or consistency, you are in a good position to estimate the likelihood of success for one or another change effort. The likelihood of your success will depend on the balance between the scope and complexity of your goal, on the one hand, and the strength of the change-producing forces will have to be. On the basis of the judgments you have made concerning the attributes of each of the forces identified, you have already implicitly assessed their usefulness and dependability. You have identified which of them are to be "working forces," which are "redundant" for your purposes, and which are "unpredictable." Moreover, you have already made a tentative decision about where to focus your actions. It has become quite clear that the strength of the working forces is directly related to the potential of achieving your goal. Undoubtedly, as you were considering each force's attributes, you were implicitly exploring the actions that you might take to influence that force. It is now time for you to be more systematic in your planning efforts.

For each working force, take a sheet of paper and jot down everything that you need to do to unlock or expand it if it is a driving force, or to nullify or reduce it if it is a restraining force. Who are the critical actors who must be involved in the process? How will you reach them? How will you induce them to work with you? Are there facilitating actors you must involve first?

Force Field Balance Sheet

	The Goal or Objective

Driving Forces (for change)

ACTORS — Amenability — Consistency — Potency (H L U)

1
2
3
4
5

	The Problem Situation or Need

(against change) Restraining Forces

1
2
3
4
5

ACTORS — Amenability — Consistency — Potency (H L U)

Critical and Facilitating Actors

A
B
C
D
E
X — Me, our group or organization

You may also wish to reexamine some of the less predictable or unpredictable forces. The ones with which you will be most concerned are those that may be low in consistency but are nevertheless high on potency. Which of these must you address? Are some likely to be more consistent under certain circumstances, or times of the year, than others?

If you are like most of us, chances are that you will not be able to answer all these questions by yourself. You know from experience that without involving others, your access to important information and to creative ideas may be limited. And without their active involvement, a change effort may be less than successful.

Which critical actors, if any, should be involved in the force field analysis process? Which facilitating actors should be involved? Should you work with others first in identifying the facilitating and critical actors? With whom? Should facilitating and critical actors be involved in the analytic aspects of the process or only at sme later stage in the change process.

SUGGESTIONS FOR FURTHER READING

Richard Beckhard, *Organizational Development: Strategies and Models*. Reading, MA: Addison-Wesley, 1969.

George Brager and Stephen Holloway, *Changing Human Service Organizations*. New York: Free Press, 1978.

Donald F. Harvey and Donald R. Brown, *An Experimental Approach to Organizational Development* (Second Edition). Englewood Cliffs, NJ: Prentice-Hall, 1981.

Arthur H. Kuriloff, *Organizational Development for Survival*. Washington, DC: American Management Association, 1972.

Kurt Lewin, "Frontiers in Group Dynamics: Concepts, Methods, and Realities in Social Science." *Human Relations*, 1 (June 1974): 5-42.

Kurt Lewin, *Field Theory in Social Science*. New York: Harper & Row, 1951.

Allen Pincus and Anne Minahan, *Social Work Practice: Model and Method*. Itasca, IL: Peacock, 1973.

7. GAMING
Making Believe for Real

ILLUSTRATIONS FROM PRACTICE

Illustration 7.1:
A Family Builds a Bridge

As far as I'm concerned, one of the best ways to get at the real relationships that exist in the family when you are in the artificial environment of a therapeutic session is to give family members real tasks to perform. If the tasks are engrossing enough, family members are likely to forget the therapist's presence and recapitulate patterns observable in the home. That's why I like using games. I'm careful to select games that have relatively open and unstructured roles, so that the participants can play the roles the way they think is appropriate. One of my favorites is to assign family members the responsibility to build a bridge. It has to span two chairs in my office. The materials are a box of tinker toys, and the instructions are simple. They have fifteen minutes to plan what they're going to build and how they're going to build it, and they have thirty minutes for building.

But then I add some complications. During the building process itself, no family member can use more than one hand at a time. As many hands as there are people in the room can be involved in the process, but participants can only use their left or right hands. If they're going to participate, therefore, they'll find it essential to interact with someone else.

The diagnostic results are phenomenal. Not only do I learn something about who works with whom and who stimulates what kinds of tensions and how family members respond to stress, but the family members make similar discoveries— about themselves and about each other.

When I use this activity, I generally schedule a two-hour session. So much new material is surfaced, it's invariably hard to come to a close. The emotions are high because people are playing for real. But my patients don't seem to leave angry or resentful toward each other. They know they are not playing for keeps.

Illustration 7.2: Locking Into A Pattern

I often use the same tool to assess management capacities as I use for assessing collegial relationships in a work unit. I have people involved in building a bridge or a tower with tinker toys. Sometimes, when there are large numbers of people involved, I'll break them into smaller work teams of six to eight.

The challenge is to build a tower of a certain height or a bridge that will span a given distance and hold three or four pounds of weight. The materials have to be properly distributed, and points are subtracted for materials left unused.

What I'm looking for are the ways in which participants plan, share responsibilities (including decision making), and initiate actions. I want to know who's a take-hold person, who is imaginative, and who can share comfortably. And I want to know whether the male participants are as comfortable in working with women as with men, and vice versa.

Almost invariably, I have found that people impose on the game their own perceptions of reality and attempt to deal with the stress of being given a challenge to complete in a given amount of time, by reverting to known patterns.

For example, in an assessment lab in which we were testing people for middle-management roles, one of the participants immediately took charge of the bridge-building activity. He directed everybody else into the performance of various tasks.

But he moved ahead like a bull in a china shop, without any plan and without providing anybody an opportunity to give feedback. Several of the participants soon lost interest and could be seen wandering around or gazing out the window. One bridge after another was designed, none of which could hold the required weight. While members of the group were annoyed with the group's "martinette," they hesitated to speak up. He's a senior member at the agency and well respected by his supervisors. He's also a member of the City Council and he's highly regarded outside the agency for his involvement in civic affairs. But the fact that he's a lousy manager was obvious to anyone who cared to look.

Illustration 7.3: Double Header

In the southeastern section of a corn belt state, sixty representatives of senior citizens' groups, social agencies, and civic associations were brought together by the staff of an area agency on aging to establish areawide priorities for the coming year. The results of their efforts were to be integrated into an area plan to be submitted to the governor's office. Before they had finished drinking their coffee and being introduced, they found themselves playing TURN-ON, a gamed simulation of the planning process.

As the morning wore on, they analyzed data on needs and available resources, studied federal and state funding guidelines, and began the process of establishing local priorities. Some participants became embroiled in a political process of give-and-take. A number formed coalitions aimed at the development of specific service programs. By the end of the morning, they had designed the outlines of an area plan and had written seven program proposals.

About a week later, in a large northeastern metropolitan community, twenty psychiatrists were involved in a very similar process. Attracted to a workshop on grantsmanship, they found themselves playing the Mental Health Planning Game. As they concerted their available money, political influence, and organizational energy, they too found themselves entering into coalitions leading to the design or expansion of service programs and to the coordination of these services.

"Hold on here," one of the psychiatrists interjected during the postplaying debriefing session. "We're not playing the right game. If we're going to design new programs and services, they might as well be relevant to our own county. Let's find out what the issues are that we should be addressing." The participants then began sorting through the issue cards that had been used to stimulate program design. They discarded those that were not relevant to their own community and wrote up new issue descriptions focusing on the problems that they felt required attention. The trainer then asked them who the participants thought cared about these issues. This led to identifying the appropriate roles to be performed in the new game. "And what kinds of resources do they each have access to?" he asked.

A new, locality-relevant version of the game was quickly designed. Participants played it that afternoon, exploring the range of alternative mental health programs and services and identifying those that were most likely to be funded through a mix of public- and private-sector sources.

GAMED SOCIAL SIMULATIONS

The practitioners in vignettes 1 and 2 were describing different uses of the same bridge-building game. The groups in the third vignette also had a single game in common. They were playing variations of COMPACTS, A COMmunity Planning and ACTion Simulation.[1] COMPACTS is a social simulation—an

1. The original version of COMPACTS was published by Gamed Simulations, Incorporated and is still available from GSI, Box 1747 FDR Station, New York, NY 10022. Other variations are also available. One is found in Armand Lauffer, *Social Planning at the Community Level* (Englewood Cliffs, NJ: Prentice-Hall, 1978), Chapter 17 (The Inter-Agency Cooperation Game). Another is Armand Lauffer, *Resources: For Child Placement and Other Human Services* (Beverly Hills, CA: Sage Publications, 1979), Chapter 11 (RFP—Resources For Permanence). The fourth version is found in Armand Lauffer, *Doing Continuing Education and Staff Development* (New York: McGraw-Hill), Chapter 23 (*Contract: The Continuing Education Training and Action Game*). Still another variation of COMPACTS is found in this chapter.

international game, but a deadly serious game. Its rules determine (1) the extent to which players can communicate with each other, (2) the nature of the agreements they can enter into, (3) the rewards they can seek for themselves or for sharing with each other, and (4) the formal or casual relationships between their actions and the outcomes.

In COMPACTS they assume the roles of community organizers and social planners, community influentials, agency administrators, funders, and consumers of social services. They form action coalitions to press for needed changes in service delivery systems or to block change efforts detrimental to their interests or to those of their constituencies. They write proposals, calculate the costs and benefits of their actions, and reward or punish other actors for their behavior.

COMPACTS is a *gamed social simulation.* Like most games, it includes players who make decisions and who interact with each other. Their behavior is governed by both formal and informal rules and is oriented toward achieving a certain outcome—an outcome that maximizes rewards and minimizes loss or punishment.

As in role playing, another form of social simulation, participants are sometimes called actors. They perform tasks and are involved in role-related transactions with the other actors in their "task environments." Unlike actors in a more traditional role-playing situation, however, participants in a play of COMPACTS and in other "gamed" simulations are only minimally concerned with *expressing* the way they feel or think. Their behavior tends to be *instrumental.* Like players in any game, their decisions and actions are oriented toward the accomplishment of defined objectives. These actions are limited by the *moves* permitted by the game's rules.

As in the real world, the criteria for "winning" may not always be so clear. Gamed social simulations are more properly identified as *gamelike* than as pure games. Some players may end up winning by one set of rules, some by another. A win strategy may be high-risk for large stakes or low-risk for smaller stakes. It may require cooperative or conflict-oriented tactics.

Players act within a social environment created by the structure of the simulation exercise: an environment containing other players representing people, groups, organizations, or social and economic forces. It is an environment governed by certain rules that permit contingent responses of the environment to the actions of individuals. It is also an environment that is created anew by the participants during each play.

Participants *play,* but they *make believe for real.* The play of a gamed social simulation reveals a real-world structure or process that the designers wish to teach or investigate. They include analogues of the real world, selected variables in a patterned and ordered arrangement. They include imbalances in power and access to scarce resources, as in real social system. There is seldom anything "fair" about these simulations as games. Players need not start off with the same amounts of resources; they have varying access to information and may find themselves peripheral to the processes of policy formation through circumstances or through lack of skill. As in real social systems, rewards and win criteria may also be variable. It is possible for many players, indeed all, to come out ahead—in accordance with their own standards of success. All, or most, may lose.

Players face predicaments that may be fortuitous or that may have been anticipated or even planned. These predicaments may become obstacles to individuals or to groups of players, or they may become opportunities by which players gain advantage for themselves, for some constituency, or for the system in its entirety. Players are constantly forced to make decisions, to establish priorities. Each decision and each action may have consequences for subsequent decisions and actions. Environmental factors outside the control of the players may act to upset player strategies or may bolster players' efforts to achieve goals. Strategies may result in competitive efforts, in collaborations and cooperative arrangements, in direct and indirect payoffs, and in outright conflict.

These processes will affect the equilibrium or imbalance of the system; they will affect the extent to which the system will maintain itself, change, or deteriorate. Just as real systems grow and decline, at various stages during the play of a game the simulated system may grow or degenerate, expand or contract, stabilize or fall into disharmony.

DEFINITIONS

Games and simulations like the bridge-building activity and COMPACTS can be used to teach participants the rules and techniques of social interaction. It may be helpful for me to define the words "simulation" and "game." A simulation is something that assumes the appearance of or acts like something else; it is an analogue of a real-world object or phenomenon. Examples of physical simulations include the wind tunnel, the Link Trainer, the dummies used in automobile accident testing, and so on. There are also social simulations. In these, the participants act as if they were performing tasks and interacting in other situations. Role play or sociodrama activities are good examples of the social simulations familiar to most human service workers. They are, however, not gamelike, because the performance of the actors involved is not necessarily rule-governed. The performance of a player in a game, by contrast, is always rule-governed.

A game, conceptually, is nothing more than a set of rules. During the play of a game, participants are involved in a set of events that are governed by those rules. Pure games include *move* rules and *termination* rules; both are very much interwoven with each other.

The move rules govern player behavior. There are three types: (1) those that govern personal choice, (2) those that represent chance, and (3) those that permit partial choice—partial chance moves. Termination rules include the game's win criterion or criteria, determine the rewards and penalties attached to different moves, and may imply the relationships between actions and outcomes. The reader will recognize, in these distinctions, the components of strategy that can be used to inform human service practice at a number of levels. There are other components as well.

THE COMPONENTS OF GAME DESIGN

Rules are but one of four components of game design. The other components are roles, scenarios, and facilitating mechanisms. Each will receive separate treatment.

Yet, the rules are central. They establish the procedures by which the game is to be played (the order of play), the behavioral constraints imposed on players as well as player obligations, the environmental responses to player actions, the manner in which conflict or impasse is resolved, the objectives for each player or coalition of players, and, by implication, who has won when the game is over.

Among the move rules that govern *personal choice* there are those that may determine the extent to which players can communicate with each other and the nature of that communication (whether or not they can enter into permanent and/or time-bound agreements), the nature of allowable exchange or transaction between players (direct exchanges and side arrangements, economic exchanges and obligatory agreements), and the amounts and types of information and other resources available to each of the players.

At times, personal choices are affected by *chance* events. Chance events may limit personal choices. Thus, in COMPACTS, randomly chosen "news events" cards may be designed to limit the range of issues upon which players can act, to increase or deplete their available resources, or to specify the other players with whom they must enter into cooperative or competitive relationships.

In some games, certain activities represent "partial chance" and "partial choice" moves. For example, in the act of throwing a dart, if the shooter were to be standing directly in front of the board at arm's reach, he or she would be in a position to choose exactly where to place the dart. There would be little chance involved. But if the shooter moved further away from the board, the choice of where to shoot might be only one of the factors determining where the dart might hit the board. Unlike the flip of a coin or the roll of a single die, which represents a completely random or chance move, the shooting of the dart always includes some choice. But it may also include a great deal of chance. The further away one is from the dart board, the "chancier" it gets that one will hit what one is aiming at.

Chance, however, can be mediated by both skill and access. Standing close to the board is one example of access. Using a blowgun or some other mechanical device that helps aim or propel the dart increases one's access. The more practice and skill one has, the more likely it is that distance (lack of access) will recede in importance. There are some important lessons here to be learned about real life. Most people are successful to the extent that they have access and skill. The parallels to real-life situations are obvious, particularly when one considers the plight of the educationally and socially disadvantaged. It is obvious in observing a playing session of COMPACTS. Some players may be closer to funders because of their role descriptions or may be more skillful in presenting their plans to funders and others. For them, the likelihood of increasing their resources or getting new projects funded may be much easier than for others. In COMPACTS, the start-up of new projects can be considered among the payoffs of the game. Others may relate to the kinds of projects developed and clients served. In some cases, rewards may be valued in terms of the power and prestige accorded an individual player for being able to halt or block a project's development.

These payoffs are embodied in the *termination rules.* These rules may include (1) rewards and punishments, (2) formal causal relationships between the actions of players and the outcomes of a game, and (3) final win criteria.

Without termination rules, there would be no motivation for players to structure their rule interactions along instrumental behavioral patterns. There would be no game, only a role-play simulation of an expressive nature. Termination rules, however, need not be fully developed by the game designer. There is some value to having the players decide what to play for during the course of play itself.

The absence of clear-cut win criteria puts each player into a quandary: "Should I play for maximum benefit for myself, or should I care about the welfare of the community or how other players will think of me?" The choice between cooperation and conflict may become an issue that is never fully resolved during play, simulating real-life dilemmas.

Finally, the absence of clear-cut win criteria makes the content of the playing experience, rather than its outcome, of central importance. In games that are clearly won or lost, players may only remember who won or what the final score was.

The participants in games are called "players." The participants in simulations are called "actors." They both perform "roles." In gamed simulations, the actors/players occupy certain statuses and perform the roles that are associated with those statuses.

According to Merton, in any social system, "each social status has its organized complement of role-relationships which can be thought of as comprising a role-set." Thus, in COMPACTS, a *consumer* of social services (the status occupied by a player) must play out his or her relationship not only to the worker in a social agency, but also to all the other actors/players with whom he or she comes into role-related contact (community workers, community influentials, funders, and other consumers who occupy a similar status). These are all members of his or her role set.

Each actor/player occupying a particular status may be involved in a set of relationship with all the members of his or her role set. They, in turn, may be involved in many relationships with each other. The patterned behavior that emerges from those interactions form the structure of a social system. Think about a soccer game. Imagine the goalie playing on the field by himself, executing all the moves possible during a game. His behavior, because it would be unrelated to others in the role set, might be interpreted a psychotic. This is an important point for the designers of a game or the educator who uses one.

The social system of a gamed social simulation is a sample of the infinitely more complex "world out there." In most instances, the players hold only a single status and are required to respond only to the role set relevant to that status. Nevertheless, diverse expectations of all members of a role set may result in considerable variety of interaction. Thus, one can expect each play of the game to be different.

What emerges from this complex interaction is a scenario. For some gamed social simulations, a partial scenario is designed in advance. It indicates something about the system within which action is to take place and provides information about the various players and the circumstances that led up to the current situation. The scenario is never fully designed, however, until the end of the play.

This may become clear when one thinks about chess or poker. While there may be an infinite number of possible scenarios, no scenario exists until the play of a particular game ends. All of the scenarios of previously played championship chess games, for example, are known and recorded in various libraries. It would not be difficult for anyone to get access to the scenarios of all of Bobby Fisher's championship games.

In a properly designed simulation, the designer provides the context within which play takes place, when any of the players can impact on the scenario as it unfolds. Players can influence the development of the scenario through the choices they make and the skill they can bring to bear on those choices.

Facilitating mechanisms make it possible to play the game. In football, it is quite obvious that play could not proceed without a ball any more than poker could proceed without a deck of cards. In gamed simulations, facilitating mechanisms might include reporting forms, applications for proposals, timing devices that keep the players attuned to the weeks or months that are passing, and so on.

These mechanisms do more than facilitate action, however. They also simulate things, events, and processes. A deck of cards, each with randomized instructions or responses to player actions, might simulate members of the role set who are not physically present at the play of the game. They might also be used to simulate chance events, just as might the role of the dice and the use of a table of random numbers. Facilitating mechanisms may include chips that represent the variety of different resources needed to play. These mechanisms can be used to structure interaction, to stimulate innovation, to point out the real and the possible.

USING GAMED SOCIAL SIMULATIONS AS ASSESSMENT TOOLS

I am certain you will have recognized the many ways in which games, like COMPACTS, can be used for training and decision making purposes. Our concern here, however, is with their use as diagnostic or assessment tools. I have found them extraordinarily helpful in assessing problems, interpersonal interactions, and alternative strategies: (1) during the course of play itself, (2) in the postplay discussion, and (3) in the game design or redesign process. Let's explore each of these possibilities. We will start with game play.

Gamed simulations disallow (or at least penalize) passivity; they literally propel players into becoming what Dewey called the "active learner." Players are quickly drawn into a web of actions and interactions in which they are faced with problems to solve and predicaments to overcome. The uninvolved is soon buffeted by the enthusiasm of other players or by their need for his or her resources. It is virtually impossible to play without constantly assessing what is and what is likely to be or without making decisions about what out to be.

Effective games transverse the dictions between consumatory and instrumental experiences. This helps overcome the gap between knowledge learned and knowledge transferred.

Too often, knowledge gained through class or in-service training is lost because of the delay in opportunity for application. In a gaming session, however, feedback is immediate. Knowledge and insights gained are used on the spot rather than being merely stored up for some future use. Participants have an opportunity to solve problems as well as to learn how they are solved.

Because players become immersed in the structure of a system, they may come to understand the connections between components of the system and linkages between subsystems. Because they are called upon to perform or to direct the functions of the system, they may develop a confidence in their ability to cope with complexity. To the extent that a simulation is empirically based, participants may learn facts about how a system operates, who controls it, and what its functions are. To the extent that it is based on some theoretic construct, players may learn about the processes by which the system is modified or maintains itself.

Although these lessons are not automatically learned through playing a game, by reducing large-scale competitive and cooperative processes to an encompassable scale manipulable by the participants, gamed simulations can expose the dynamics of social interaction with a lucidity rarely achieved through conventional teaching means. This, however, is not without some risk. Every play of a game is different, the designer's construct serving as a loose script and the players creating the performance anew each time. In a very real sense, players invent and reinvent the social system simulated during each run of the simulation. Thus, every participant in a gaming session is likely to learn something else, based on personal experience.

This postplay discussion, or debriefing session, is where most assessments usually take place. This is where participants can examine what happened, how it happened, and whether it should have happened. Typically, postplay discussion includes an examination of the following:[2]

(1) *The rules governing play activities and determination rules or win criteria.* To what extent do these reflect reality? Are these the rules that govern our behavior in the family, in our agency, in the community? If some people play by other rules, can we still be engaged in the game together? Are different participants playing by different determination rules, that is, are they each concerned with the same win criteria? How does that simulate reality in our agency, in our family, in our neighborhood? Are the rules functional; could they be changed so as to facilitate interaction and increase satisfaction (winning)?

2. For a more complete discussion, see Armand Lauffer, *The Aim of the Game: A Primer on the Use and Design of Gamed Social Simulations* (New York: Gamed Simulations, Inc.), 1973.

(2) *The player roles.* Were participants satisfied with the roles they performed in the game? How might the rules be modified? Were participants' roles shaped by the expectations of others in their role sets? Did people perform their roles appropriately, that is, were they involved in the right kinds of issues, or were they performing the tasks expected of a particular role encumbent? What implications does this have for family interactional patterns, work group relationships, supervisory and management staff functions, the interactions between community leaders and others?

(3) *The scenario.* Did the scenario, as it unfolded, reflect a typical pattern of behavior and action in the system being simulated? What other scenarios were possible? How could a shift in the resources allocated to different players result in a different scenario? Had people performed their roles differently, what might have changed during the course of playing? If different incumbents had performed given roles, what might have changed? What implications do these answers have for community, organization, family, or small group behavior?

(4) *The facilitating mechanisms and materials.* Were there any partial chance/partial choice mechanisms in the game, and how did they enhance play? Were the forms to be filled out, Tinker Toy materials, or other mechanisms (like dice and spinners or boards) an adequate analogue to some phenomenon or material in the real world? Would a change in their design or availability have affected changes in the scenario? By analogy, what implications does this have for small group, family, organization, or community actions?

Perhaps most of all, games can be valuable assessment tools by the very fact that someone has to design them. By using gaming activities as opportunities to build and test models to examine the cost and benefits of adopting alternative strategies, it becomes possible to test one's notions of both structure and function. It is possible, for example, to uncover the extent to which people are committed to a particular course of action or final plan, to inject new information about problems and needs and examine the extent to which that information may shape decision making, and to examine the outcomes and costs of alternative strategies and tactics. It is a good deal cheaper to do it with games than to do it in the real world, where people are playing for keeps.

In designing a game, it is possible to explore what is and what is likely to be and to design and test a model of what ought to be.

TWO GAMES FOR YOUR USE

The following pages include instructions for two games: a variation of the bridge-building exercise, described in Illustrations 7.1 and 7.2, and LINK, a variation of COMPACTS that deals with interagency linkages and coordination. You will find that it articulates closely with the interorganizational linkage exercises in Chapter 2.

Read the instructions first. Consider how you might adapt or modify the instructions for use in your particular situation. The instructions for the bridge-building game presume several playing groups working simultaneously. Similar versions have been used for assessing work group interactions, morale, and job satisfaction. How might you modify it for examining planning capabilities, managerial skills, or communication styles in your agency? How might you modify it for use in family treatment or in work with disturbed adolescents in a congregational living situation?

Activity 7.1: Bridge Building

Read the instructions carefully and modify them for your own purposes. You will need one box of Tinker Toys (the "engineer" size) for each playing group. Between four and nine can work with a single box of Tinker Toys. The "Instructions to Players" that follow may be handed out to participants with the box of Tinker Toys. I have found it better, however, to read it or to explain it aloud. It takes about five minutes to give all the instructions needed.

Instructions to Players

Your task is to build a bridge with all the materials in the Tinker Toy box given to your group so that it will span an open space while carrying a load of five pounds of more, following the rules spelled out below and in accordance with established performance measures.

(1) Take up to thirty minutes for planning. This requires that you:
   (a) decide who will be responsible for which tasks (that is, allocate responsibilities)
   (b) work out your design
   (c) prepare your materials
   (d) establish the criteria by which you want your final product evaluated, and write them down (see *Criteria,* below)

   If you finish in less than thirty minutes, you may begin building.

(2) Take up to forty-five minutes for building (or more if you incorporate part of your planning time; but in no case may planning and building take up more than seventy-five minutes in toto. You must:
   (a) use up all the materials in your box unless you don't mind being penalized (see *Penalties,* below)
   (b) span an open space at least twelve inches wide (much like a bridge might span a river or highway)
   (c) make certain that no individual player uses more than one hand at a time for construction activities (two or more players can work together, but each can use only one of his or her hands), or your group may suffer a penalty.

(3) In establishing the *criteria* by which you would like to have your results evaluated, allocate 100 points in any way you wish to the following, but no criterion item can be worth less than 5 points or more than 50. Add other items you feel are relevant. (Note: the "judges" will also be developing criteria. Judgments will be made on the basis of a joint scoring system.)

   (a) aesthetics   _____
   (b) form follows function   _____
   (c) group cooperation and task coordination   _____
   (d) _____   _____
   (e) _____

                                                         _____

(4) Although you might score 100 points, there are also penalties. You will lose:

   (a) 100 points if your bridge does not hold five pounds or if it does not span a full twelve inches

   (b) points for any of the materials in your box that are not used up, as follows: 3 points for each connector wheel; 2 points each for connector cylinder and the longest sticks; 1 point each for all other items; and 5 points for every time a player is detected using two hands.

Postplay Activities

(1) Now it is time for judging. This should take about ten minutes.

   (a) Arrive at a composite scoring system by adding up your own group's scoring mechanism (you worked this out in relation to the criteria you established in response to item 3 of the instructions) to that of the judges (those who will be evaluating your efforts). Then divide the total on each criterion item by 2. This is now the composite scoring system. For example:

		Your Group	The Judges	Total	Composite
a.	aesthetics				
b.	form follows function	20	40	60	30
c.	group cooperation	50	10	60	30
d.	_____	20	40	40	
e.	_____	5		5	2½
f.	_____	5		5	2½
g.	_____		20	20	10
			10	10	5
	Totals	100	100	200	100

   (b) You are now ready to have your project evaluated and to evaluate that of another group. The group evaluating your project will use your composite scoring system. You will use the other group's. What is this akin to?

   Remember: after the criteria have been applied, you must still subtract penalty points as outlined under item 4 of the rules.

   Post the scores for each group on the board.

(2) Finally, take about thirty minutes for postplay discussion. We sometimes call this debriefing.

   (a) Elect someone to lead the discussion and one or two persons to record the major points made. Initial recording might go on the board so that the group can correct any errors or add to major issues addressed. A more polished summary of two or three pages should be prepared for review at a later time. (Note: if you wish, you may divide this task among more people.)

(b) Use the following as your beginning agenda. Add more items, if you wish.

- Why did one group score higher than another? Are the reasons to be found in the scoring mechanisms used, in the products or in the way they were built, or in the biases of the judges?

- If things worked well in your group, what were the contributing factors? How about the factors that worked against goal attainment? How did each of the groups compare in relation to these factors?

- What were the factors that influenced the way members of each group contributed? Did gender, experience, attitude, social status outside of class influence people's role behavior and their sense of commitment to the activity? Their sense of satisfaction from the activity (both the product and the process)?

- How might this activity be used for assessment purposes in your agency or with some other organization with which you are familiar? What modifications would it need? How would the participants have to be prepared?

Activity 7.2: LINK: Locating Information and Network Kinetics[3] (a Variation of COMPACTS)

For this activity, you will need three sets of written materials and enough of each for all participants. These materials are (1) the *Glossary of Linking Mechanisms* (see Chapter 2), (2) the *Issues That Might Be Addressed Through Interorganizational Linkages* pack found on pages 158-162, and (3) the *LINK*

---

3. Those readers interested in delving more deeply into issues pertaining to interagency exchanges will be interested in a recent Sage Human Service Guide. See Robert Rossi, Kevin Gilmartin, and Charles Dayton, *Improving Interagency Coordination* (Beverly Hills, CA: Sage Publications, 1982).

Proposal Form on pages 162-163. Feel free to photocopy these materials directly from the book or to have them retyped in larger print. While you are at it, consider modifying or adding to the glossary if there are other linkages that make more sense to the issues and organizations with which you are concerned. Consider also adding to or otherwise modifying the issues that might be addressed.

In order to play the game, you will also need "play checks" or sufficient play money for a single round of play. Depending on your own judgment (read over the issues first), you might want between $200,000 and $1,000,000 in play money. You will also need enough paper or poker chips in the colors indicated under item 4 on the Proposal Form to give each participant between zero and ten. You can decide on how many you think are appropriate. In effect, I am now involving you in the process of game design.

You will also have to decide on how many persons should play and what roles they should perform. Normally, LINK can be played comfortably with between fifteen and thirty-five players. If you have enough roles, you can accommodate more. It is not effective if fewer than fifteen participate. Consider giving out roles to persons in the following categories.

- *Agency administrators:* public welfare, community mental health, child guidance clinic, vocational rehabilitation, CETA, public schools, county hospital.

- *Community influentials:* president of the Council of Jewish Women, president of the Jaycees, union leader, church leader, member of the city council, industrialist.

- *Consumer organizations:* Grey Panthers, Parents of Retarded Children, neighborhood association, Latino coalition.

- *Funding officials:* neighborhood development block grant corporation, community foundation, United Fund, state department of health.

Modify or add to this list to reflect the kinds of organizations and individuals that are relevant to your particular situation. Now consider the extent of their resources in terms of (1) *money* to allocate (checks or play money); (2) necessary *information* (units of information can be simulated by white poker chips, or you might prefer actually to give people information relevant to plan making on 3×5 cards); (3) *personal energy* (can be simulated with blue poker chips); (4) *political influence* (units can be simulated with red poker chips); and (5) *legitimacy or legality* (can be simulated with transparent poker chips).

Preparing for Play

(1) Draw up a role badge (stick-on tape will do) for each player. Add or subtract players depending on how many people will be available. You can comfortably go as low as fifteen or as high as sixty. If you have more players than roles, ask people to double up (this works especially well for funders).

(2) Put each role badge into a plastic sandwich bag together with a limited number of strategic resource chips. These can be poker chips, bits of colored paper, lego blocks, or the like. For each type of strategic resource, you will need a different color. The following is illustrative. Any set of colors might work.

Money and credit	=	checks or play money
Information	=	white
Personal energy	=	blue
Political influence	=	red
Legitimacy and legality	=	gray or transparent

Feel free to modify the number of resource chips you put in each baggie. Experiment to see what works best and to approximate your view of the situation in your setting. But remember, life is not always fair; some players will not have the same access to strategic resources as others may.

(3) You are now ready to set up your room. Arrange tables so that each category of players sits at one or two tables. Lay out the plastic baggies with the name badges and resource chips on the

tables where appropriate. A typical setup might look like the following. Process observers may be scattered about.

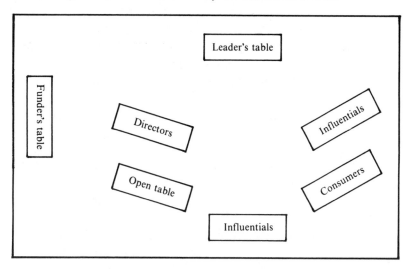

Put up a wall chart telling people which color is used to designate each strategic resource (see instruction 2 above). Have at least as many chairs as baggies, with role badges and chips at each table. Have extra newsprint or board and chalk available for players to use. Duplicate twenty to thirty copies of the instructional materials that follow, if you feel this will be helpful. If not, be sure to duplicate the Contract Proposal Form. Then duplicate two or three copies of the Priorities Form for each funder.

Introducing Players to the Rules of the Game

(1) As players come into the room, greet them and ask them to find a role in which they are interested. Then ask them to pin or stick on a role badge and sit down at the table where they find that badge.

(2) When everyone is seated, introduce them to LINK somewhat as follows (using your own words):

Welcome to LINK: Locating Information and Network Kinetics. Notice that you have several proposal forms on your tables (show them one). *These will be used to get interagency activities organized in our area. Before we go much further, it would be good to know who will be playing.*

Turn to one table at a time, and ask each person to stand up and introduce himself of herself. For example, a player might say, "I'm Morgan Schwartz, director of the community mental health center." A second might indicate that she is an adoption worker with the county. In other words, people should introduce themselves according to the roles designated on their badges, not their real-life roles.

After introductions have been made, continue:

Now that we know who we are, let's find out what kinds of strategic resources we've got to work with. Notice that there are colored chips in your baggies. Each color represents a particular resource.

Show them the chart, and explain that these resources are needed to get a new program or project off the ground. Funders who have access to money and credit, for example, will want to be certain that a local group that wants to start a new service has access to other resources, such as energy and legitimacy.

Our challenge will be to design program plans that link organizations more effectively around issues of mutual concern. Look over the issues packet we have put on each table. Examine the Glossary of Potential Linking Mechanisms.

To play LINK you'll have to find others in the community who have similar interests. Decide what you think is needed and start designing a new service or program to deal with those needs, but do check on what the funding priorities are for this year.

Funders should be thinking of their priorities. What kinds of programs are on your priority list? To whom will you give a grant? What regulations regarding consumer involvement, budgeting, or evaluations do you have? You should decide on your priorities during the first fifteen minutes of play. You may wish to list your priorities and regulations on a piece of newsprint for everyone to see. Some funders develop these priorities only after they have surveyed needs and interests. Others have them ready right at the start of the fiscal year. Still others are quite often flexible, prefer-ring not to specify all their priorities. Which one are you?

Other players should check some of these questions out too. If you organize and submit a proposal to a funder, be sure it is complete and clearly written. The more actors interested in con-tributing to your purpose, the more people in your coalition, and the more resources you collect, the stronger your case for funding. Anyone can start up the process leading to design of a project, but you probably won't be successful without collaboration with others.

This is a resource orchestration exercise. Funders are going to be interested in how well you've been able to orchestrate local resources before they allocate funds. Get others you are working with on a program design to commit their resources to that program. In some cases a federal or state funder may require a 25 percent local match in terms of dollars. At other times funders will want to know that you will be able to provide in-kind matches through facilities and personnel and that there is a good deal of support for your project. This support might be represented through your collection of energy and political influence chips. A funder may not be terribly impressed with the energy you put behind the proposal if you have no access to political influence or legitimacy. In some cases you'll need a balance. In others you'll need to concentrate more on one or another strategic resource.

Before they actually begin to play, walk participants through each section of the proposal form. Then tell them that the fiscal year is sixty minutes long and that you will let them know periodically how much time has elapsed.

Any questions? OK. The fiscal year has begun!

Coaching During Play

Once play begins, your role is one of coach or enabler. Answer questions, but don't tell players what to do. Ask them how they would act if they were playing the role on their badges in a real-life situation or ask them to imagine how a funder would evaluate their proposal if a section of the proposal were not clearer, and so on. Announce the time every few minutes. Warn players when there are only two minutes left. (Funders won't accept proposals after the end of the fiscal year.) Then stop play.

Postplay Discussion

When play is over, participants will be anxious to talk about what happened. You might want to focus on some or all of the following:

(1) Which linkage plans were successful, and which ones were not? Why? Ask players who worked on a successful proposal to explain why things worked the way they did. Ask the same of those who were not successful. Probe for real-life parallels and for practice principles that might reform action at work.

(2) Whose proposals were best. Why? Because of their thoroughness? Because of their objectives? Because of the support they engendered? Would such a project work in your (the participants') communities?

(3) Did you feel each actor played his or her role appropriately? Focus on a certain actor, such as a funder, a representative of a consumer group, or perhaps an agency administrator. Find principles that participants might use in trying to make friends and influence people in a real situation.

Relate subsequent discussion to the interests of the group playing, staff developers, administrators in the host organization, and so forth.

Issues That Might Be Addressed Through Interorganizational Linkages

Youth unemployment. Many of the teens who have applied for summer job training and placement come from families who have been longtime recipients of Aid to Families with Dependent Children. Others are the children of union members who have lost their jobs due to plant shutdowns. Some are school dropouts, and about 10 percent have police records. Their level of skill and their attitudes about work vary considerably.

Independent living. The imminent closure of many public institutions is likely to inundate local agencies with requests for service from the mentally ill, the developmentally disabled, and the handicapped. Many of these people have the potential for independent living, but not without the necessary social, economic, and home-care supports.

Hard-to-place children. An increasingly large number of children and youth live in situations that, at best, could be described as temporary. Permanency planning has been most difficult for the developmentally disabled, for children of interracial parents, and for older children and youth who have already spent a year or more in foster homes. Group home arrangements are only partially satisfactory and sometimes create difficulties for the neighborhoods in which the children live and the schools to which they are sent.

No place to die. A hospice was recently established for the terminally ill, but few people knew of it, and few hospitals, physicians, or social agencies relate to it. The hospice is in danger of closing because of underutilization and underfunding.

Violence on the rise. Incidents of domestic violence have increased with the rise of unemployment and with greater awareness that one need not be victimized by others or by one's own emotions forever. Violence on the streets has also increased, but not at as rapid a rate as people's fears of being mugged or sexually assaulted. Neither preventive nor corrective programs are adequate to deal with the actual and potential victims and perpetrators of violence.

Inflation and retail gougers. Inflation, combined with high rates of unemployment and cutbacks in transfer payments, have combined to reduce the discretionary funds available to most community residents. Ethnic minorities and others who traditionally are at or below the poverty line have been hardest hit. Retail stores in their neighborhoods charge higher prices than those in other areas of the city. A local merchant explains that this is necessary because wholesale prices rise rapidly and because of the high incidence of theft. On the other hand, consumers complain that available merchandise is of inferior quality.

The Russians are coming. Jewish refugees from the Soviet Union have been relocated in increasing numbers in this community. While some come with considerable education, their professional training is not directly transferable to the United

States. A disproportionate number are elderly. Few, if any, speak English on arrival, and none were able to take any money or more personal possessions than they could carry out with them.

Cutbacks cut deep. Cutbacks in state and federal funding have all but resulted in the closure of crisis intervention clinics in the community, at the university, and especially in the out-county areas. Hotlines, if they operate at all, are managed by volunteers. Shelters and temporary housing facilities are overwhelmed but understaffed and underfunded.

A house is not a home. The increase in the cost of rental housing has been exceeded only by the steep rise in the cost of utilities. The building of public housing has come to a virtual standstill. The inability of middle-class people to finance the purchase of private homes has further increased the demand for reasonable rental housing. In the meantime, large blocks of abandoned housing owned by HUD remain empty and unimproved. The housing situation for many inner-city residents, particularly blacks, has become desperate.

No fun this year. The settlement house has recently closed down half its programs because of a cut in United Funds allocations. The City Recreation Department is anticipating a similar cut in its ability to fund its summer park programs and is considering charging for some programs that formerly were provided at no cost.

What's the meaning of this? All local agencies are required to keep records and to maintain statistics on their programs and on the client needs they are addressing. But there is rarely any comparability between their reporting forms, nor is information routinely shared between organizations that may serve common client populations or common geographic areas.

Spaced out. The use of undercover cops to root out the drug pushers in a local high school has raised the issue of drug and alcohol abuse among teenagers in the public consciousness. Others have become concerned about drunk drivers, but few people have yet drawn the obvious connections between the two. The interrelated problems affect everyone—school officials, mental health personnel, the police, welfare council officials, unions, employers, and the general public.

The ghetto blues. The promise of the civil rights revolution has been all but forgotten as financial concerns, reductions in equal opportunity programs, and legislative attempts to limit busing have reinforced the conviction of many low-income minorities that they will continue to be systematically discriminated against. A reawakened political activism is a possibility, but for the moment there seems to be a smoldering discontent that sometimes turns itself inward and at other times erupts in uncoordinated violence.

Robotics. There is not much danger that robots will replace social workers in the provision of social services. But with decertification and with the increase of untrained workers in many agencies and the extensive use of volunteers in others, the standards for effective and for ethical practice have come under fire. Robots can do quality work, at an agreed-upon standard, and they do not suffer from stress or burnout. The same cannot be said of the all-too-human workers in the human services.

Private-sector initiatives. Everyone agrees that the private sector will have to assume greater responsibility for the support and provision of needed social services—everyone but those who work in the private sector. No one has much of a plan for inducing the private sector to become more involved or, for that matter, a clear idea of how it should be involved or in what. There's not much initiative in the private sector!

Where do we go from here? As agency capacities become more limited but demands increase, it becomes more important to know where to refer clients with special needs and how; but central referral capacities do not exist. Agencies are reluctant to accept clients improperly referred by other agencies or by private organizations and private practitioners.

We can do it better. The growth of mutual help groups is an expression of the desire on the part of many potential clients to change their status from consumer to producer and to regain some control over their own lives and conditions. But it also reflects a challenge to professionals who "haven't been there," or who may be perceived as not authentically concerned and perhaps not even capable.

LINK Proposal Form

Face sheet information

1. Title of proposal   _____

2. Organizational sponsorship or auspice   _____

---

3. Funding requested $ _____ In-kind or local match $

4. Dates _____ Project director

Project or Program Narrative

1. Objectives to be reached   2. Primary and secondary beneficiaries

3. New linkages to be established and/or existing linkages to be strengthened (refer to code-numbers and names of linkages on inventory form)

4. Resources allocated to the project by participating organizations

Participant (Organization)	Money and Credit ($)	Information (white)	Personal Energy (blue)	Political Influence (red)	Legitimacy/ Legality (transparent)

5. Evaluation procedures   6. Budget justification

*Locating Interorganizational Network Kinetics

Interorganizational Exchange Matrix

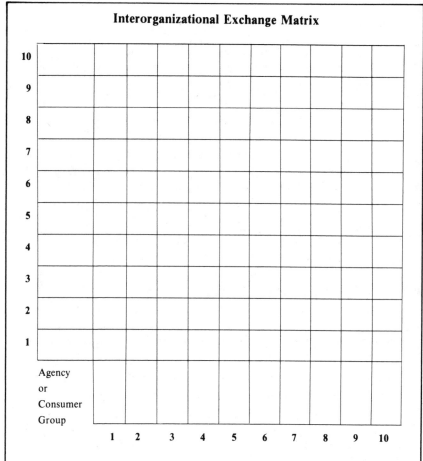

Instructions

1. List up to ten agencies and consumer groups that are or should be involved in exchange relationships with each other. Each organization will appear twice, once in a column and once in a row space. Organization 1 will appear in the appropriate locations twice, as will organizations 2, 3, 4, and so on).

2. Using black ink or pencil, indicate which linkages are currently in operation between organizations by using its code number and writing it in the appropriate square (where the two organizations by using its code number and writing it in the appropriate square (where the two organizations' rows and columns intersect). If the exchange is one-way only, so indicate by use of an arrow showing direction.

3. Using a second color ink or pencil, indicate which of those linkages should be eliminated by crossing it out and which should be improved by circling it.

4. If you have enough room on the matrix, use the second color to write in additional desired linkages. If more room is needed, use a new matrix.

WHAT'S NEXT?

Once you have played either one of these games, you will have ideas about how to modify it or tailor it to your specific purposes. In fact, the more you play them, the more ideas you'll have. No single game construct, however, can do everything. You may be interested in exploring others. There are virtually thousands of games available in the United States and Canada. They are aimed at every age and deal with every conceivable subject. The most comprehensive guide to simulations and games, Robert Horn's *Guide,* is published by Sage Publications and is listed in the suggested readings that follow. The latest edition includes complete descriptions, prices, and places from where you might order games. It also includes reviews that might help you decide whether or not the game is relevant to your interests and needs.

There's also another piece of good news. Gamers like to interact with other gamers and to share their experiences as well as their constructs. You might be interested in joining the North American Simulations and Gaming Association (NASAGA). It publishes a bimonthly magazine called *Simulation/Gaming.* NASAGA also conducts national and regional meetings. If you want to find out more, write to the organization: NASAGA, c/o COMEX, Davidson Conference Center, University of Southern California, Los Angeles, CA 90007. If you are interested in a subscription to the journal, write to *Simulation/Gaming,* Box 3039, University Station, Moscow, ID 83843.

SUGGESTIONS FOR FURTHER READING

D. C. Bell, "Simulation Games: Three Research Paradigms." *Simulations and Games,* 6 (1975) 271-278.

John G. Carlson and Michael J. Misshauk, *Introduction to Gaming: Management Decision Simulations.* New York: John Wiley, 1972.

Richard Duke, *Gaming: The Future's Language.* Beverly Hills, CA: Sage Publications, 1975.

Robert E. Horn, *The Guide to Simulation Games for Education and Training* (Third Edition). Cambridge: Information Resources, 1977.

Robert E. Horn, *The Guide to Simulations and Games* (Fourth Edition). Beverly Hills, CA: Sage Publications, 1981.

Armand Lauffer, *The Aim of the Game: A Primer on the Use and Design of Gamed Social Simulations.* New York: Gamed Simulations, 1973.

Martin Shubik (ed.), *Game Theory and Related Approaches to Social Behavior.* Huntington, VA: Krieger Publications, 1975.

8. IMAGES OF REALITY
Photography as an Assessment Tool

ILLUSTRATIONS FROM PRACTICE

Illustration 8.1: Look Who's There

Nothing triggers off associations and memories of what was and what could be or could have been more than a photograph . . . or better still, an album or collection of photographs. Early on in my work with families and with children who have been neglected or abandoned, I ask my clients to bring in their family albums. Not everyone has one, of course, But many people do keep snapshots and other visual keepsakes in boxes, drawers, and in their wallets.

The photos that people keep, and the way in which they keep them tell me (and them) more than any of a dozen talk sessions. Which child appears more often, at what age? Who are the strange people who appear once and never again? When or for what occasions are pictures taken? Who is not *there is more important than who* is. *How often, for example, have you looked at the family album and remarked that the mother or father is not present? Is that the person who is taking the picture? Is that person normally an "observer" rather than a participant, a chronicler rather than an active and integral part of the family unit? Who has the pictures and who keeps the album?*

**Illustration 8.2: What's A Good Image, Anyway,
and Who's Looking?**

*My work took me to many of the city's distinct ethnic
neighborhoods. Because of my avocational interest in
photography, I often brought my SLR along. Sometimes I
stayed on in search of good photographs after my official
business was done, prowling the streets, looking for interesting
faces, scenes reflecting the quality of life, unusual architectural
or environmental features. There was nothing particularly
scientific or systematic in my work. I was trying to make
"good" photographs from an artistic perspective. I often
returned a few days later to follow-up on an interesting "story
line," or to capture those scenes I had missed because of the
press of time or the principle reason for my original visit. A
number of unexpected experiences and insights were the
result.*

*I discovered that it is impossible to remain invisible when
intruding into someone else's neighborhood with a camera.
"Hey are you from the TV?" I would be asked by people not
familiar with long (telephoto) lenses. Or "Are you here for
Newsweek?" People wanted to know why I was interested in
them. Not wanting to appear like a "Peeping Tom" or a
tourist with his ever-present Instamatic, I replied that I was
working on photos for a book on the city's neighborhoods (an
idea I had begun toying with). "Then you're looking at the
wrong people (or places). I'll show you what the real
neighborhood is like," I was sometimes told. On a number of
occasions, particularly if someone remembered me from an
earlier visit, I was directed where to shoot if I wanted to
perceive the neighborhood from the community's, or at least
my informant's, point of view.*

*That's when I was lucky. In other instances I was told in no
uncertain terms to leave, sometimes with the threat of bodily
harm. In one situation my presence so disrupted the scene
that no photograph was either possible or desirable. I had
begun setting up to photo the informal lounging and free-
flowing banter around a vegetable stall in the farmer's market.*

My activity totally interrupted the interaction and there were angry protests regarding my presence due in part to suspicion that I might be from the "mafia." I finally persuaded the green grocer to let me take the photo. He posed stiffly, and I promised to bring him a print.

A few weeks later I returned with the print. It was very stilted and hardly reflected the dynamics I had hoped to catch. "Great," exclaimed the proud proprietor, "Look at how fresh the strawberries are!" "Terrible," exclaimed his wife, "You look like an old man." "You want to see a good picture?" she turned to me. "I'll show you one." And she pulled from a pocket in her apron a frayed and fading picture of the two of them as a young couple in Salonika. It was clear that what she wanted people to see in a photo about her husband was not what I had photographed. Like the people who wanted to show me the "real" neighborhood, she also had ideas of what was accurate or reflected well on the subject of the photo.

Later, on sorting through my slides, I began to see certain patterns that I had not noticed when on the street taking pictures. In some neighborhoods there was an active street life wherever you pointed the camera. In some, photos showed only old people. In others the streets were full of people of all ages and of many ethnic backgrounds. The photos of some neighborhoods had no sky. In some sets of photos, automobiles intruded frequently; in others they were totally absent. In some neighborhoods, windows were boarded up. The porches were full of the kinds of junk some of you would store in attics or garages. In other places, the porches were emaculate, often decorated with potted plants.

Did the outside appendage to one's home have different functions for residents in some neighborhoods than for those of others, I wondered. Could the porch and the way it is used reflect on a person's status in the community, in the public "face" he wished to present? My photos, incomplete, and unsystematic a record that they might be, were turning into a source of data; data that could be mined just as one mines folk music, field notes, cultural artifacts, unstructured interviews. What was needed was a concept, a code, and a more systematic approach to collecting data with the camera. And what was absolutely required, if the data were to be correctly interpreted, were the perceptions of knowledgeable informants . . . the residents in the neighborhoods and others.

These insights seemed so elementary that I was certain they were frivolous. After all, hadn't Jacob Riis studied neighborhood conditions and the plight of immigrant populations in New York at the turn of the century? Weren't Lewis Hine's studies of work on the mines at the turn of the century considered good sociology? And didn't Walker Evan's and Dorothea Lange's work for the Farm Security Administration in the 1930's lead to social policy changes? I began searching the professional literature for more contemporary examples. I came across a document in German describing the use of photographs to record neighborhood conditions in Munich. The approach used reminded me somewhat of Bushnell's work in Chicago almost 80 years earlier. But in the German case, the photos were blown up billboard size and exhibited on the walls of buildings in the same neighborhood. The reactions of neighborhood residences to these images were then studied and photographed.

Contemporary American literature was sparse. I did find some but not many additional studies of comparable interest. Still photography, in fact, is almost totally absent from the American sociological and social work literature . . . both as a source of data and as a tool for interpreting and conveying information. And it has virtually no place in the conduct of social work practice. But it would have in my own practice and research, I determined.

In one of the neighborhoods my Community Organization students were involved in organizing, we decided to test out the use of photography as an assessment tool that could at once inform us of where people were and what they valued, and that could be used to build critical consciousness . . . in effect to actively involve them in taking charge over the conditions we were going to photography. Here's how the project worked.

First we met with the Neighborhood Action Committee and explained what we had in mind. We wanted to get a real "picture" of what the neighborhood looked like. We would share our pictures with the committee to do as it liked—put in a neighborhood album, send to the press, use in pressuring city hall or in informing neighbors about what was expected of them in terms of upkeep. But we needed their help. As newcomers, we would need to know what kinds of pictures to collect. We needed some people who could direct us and help us decide what to take pictures of, and even walk around with us so that we wouldn't stand out so much as strangers.

Secondly, we met with the committee's volunteers and some other residents who were really in the know . . . the druggist on Chelsea Street, Mrs. Carver who had raised nine kids on the neighborhood's streets and in its schools, and some others. In effect, what they did is help us design our "shooting script." The process was no different than one might use in working with local people in the design of a needs assessment questionnaire. But it was a hell of a lot more interesting. Low income and relatively uneducated people don't have much interest in questionnaire design. But they sure got turned on by the idea of creating a neighborhood album . . . with pictures speaking for them when words couldn't quite express what they thought or felt.

We then spent several days shooting, almost always with one of our "guides" available, if we needed them. They helped in two ways. Their introductions helped eliminate the kids of suspicion and hostility we might of otherwise have encountered. And they knew where to look . . . where rats infested buildings and where dogs turned over garbage cans; where kids hung out and where drugs were sold; where mothers and pre-schoolers gathered to talk on sunny afternoons; where four neighbors or one block were fixing up their yards and porches and painting to demonstrate pride and a determination to reverse the process of decay.

After we printed our photos . . . we had about 450 prints, we sorted them out with our guides. I suppose, if we had been anthropologists, we would have called them our "native

informants," and we would have considered our work to be
an ethnographic study. But we were community organizers,
and we wanted people not only to inform us, but to use the
stimulus of our photos to make some decisions about
themselves and what they wanted to do about their
community. So we asked some very specific questions:

- If we had to pick 20 pictures to tell the story of the neighborhood
  the way it really is, which would they be?
- If we wanted to point up to the people at city hall how neglected
  our neighborhood is, which 20 would we choose?
- If we were to select the images of the way we would want our
  neighborhood to look to others, which 20 would we select?

The three questions led to selecting 49 pictures, some of
which fell into more than one category. Mrs. Carver suggested
that we weren't through yet and that other people should see
these pictures, too. That's precisely the suggestion we were
waiting for.

I won't bore you with the details. But I will tell you this.
The Neighborhood Action Committee decided to sponsor an
"open air gallery" on the outside walls of the old McCormick
plant. The building had been empty for two years. The photos
were blown up billboard size. The committee assigned
"guides" to interpret the meanings of the pictures. But the
images really spoke for themselves. The press was invited.
People for the city-wide community development corporation
came. Residents not only had a great time seeing pictures of
themselves and their homes on display, but felt proud that
outsiders were coming to the festivities and to look.

More important, the Committee had made a strong
statement about what was wrong in the neighborhood and
what their images of the future were. The comments
overheard as people looked at the photos suggested they
weren't alone in their concerns, even if not everyone agreed on
what each of the pictures really meant. That's what had to be
thrashed out at public meetings. One-hundred and thirty-eight
people came to the next public forum of the Neighborhood

Action Committee. Only twenty-three had attended the previous month's meeting.

What had started out as an effort on our part to assess local conditions had turned out to be the energizer the neighborhood needed to articulate its needs and its vision of the future.

PHOTOGRAPHY AS A TOOL

At first, it seems incredible that still photography has been almost ignored in sociological and social work research and in social work intervention. Sophisticated scientific research in such fields as astronomy, botany, chemistry, physics, medicine, architecture and engineering is almost unthinkable without photography. Yet of the social sciences, only anthropology has made extensive use of either the still or the moving photograph. The use of photos disappeared from the *American Journal of Sociology* in 1916, never to reappear. Photos are virtually absent from any and all professional social work journals. Those welfare-related journals that do publish photographs use them for illustrative rather than scientific purposes.

The application of still photography in family and individual treatment and in interventions at the organizational and community levels have been almost totally neglected. Little more attention has been given to its application in training for the human services. Perhaps the problem lies in the "image of the photo image." It is variously seen as having recreational, journalistic, commercial or artistic applications. The potential for its use in recording and describing problems, communicating and retrieving both information and feelings, increasing public awareness, and identifying the desirable is yet to be developed.

You can participate in that development. Consider one of the following possibilities:

- Helping children in adoptive or foster care settings maintain personal histories and linkages with their pasts;
- Using the family album to retrieve information in marital counseling;

- Involving neighborhood residents in photographing their own communities and then selecting those images they wish to project to the rest of the city (e.g., goal setting as part of a larger developmental or renewal effort);
- Using the photo image to help people who have difficulty in verbalizing and articulating their feelings, perceptions and ideas (disadvantaged minorities, the disabled, those with language barriers);
- Involving agency staff in defining their organizational missions and services through images that can be used to clarify the perceptions, set priorities, and communicate with clients, policy makers, and the general community.

What others can you suggest?

Consider also how photos might go beyond assessment. Effectively used, photographs can promote communion, a sense of shared identity (like a family album or class year book). They can be used to reinforce relationships, beliefs, social patterns and commitments, important factors in successful community organizing. They can promote interaction, as subjects and relevant others decide what is to be photographed, how and when, or where the photos are to be exhibited and to what end. They can be used for documentation.

They can be used for the "presentation of self" in either a natural portrayal, or an idealized portrayal. They can communicate a desired message. By raising consciousness, the possibility of action, if only on immediate and small scale changes, is likely to be enhanced. In effect, the contexts of discovery, presentation, and action are interwoven.

Activity 8.1: What's in a Picture: Doing a Content Analysis of the Family Album

Now it's your turn. In this exercise, you will have an opportunity to discover for yourself what can be uncovered in a family album. First, a few words about *content analysis*. It is a research method that can be used to uncover patterns in found or available materials. For example, one might do a content analysis of a series of letters to uncover thought patterns, emotions, political persuasions, problems, etc. If you were analyzing a packet of letters written by one of your grandparents, you might look for the number of times economic concerns, worries about children, expressions of anger and frustration, reflections on ethnic or religious identity, the naming of certain people or events occur, and at what times in the person's life or career.

One can also do a content analysis on newspaper articles, editorials, T.V. or radio news stories, Hollywood films, or any other medium in which you are seeking patterns. The same holds true for the family album. Start off by making a list of variables you are interested in finding out about. A partial list follows:

- Who appears in the pictures, how often, and at what periods in the family's development? Who is never or hardly ever in the picture?
- When are most pictures taken (summer, winter, at family events)?
- Are pictures taken outdoors or indoors more often? What kinds of backgrounds are found in the picture?
- Does the quality of picture taking change? Does the type of picture (black and white, instamatic, Polaroid) change? What meaning does this have? When does the change take place?

Select those items that are relevant to your area of concern (and others). As you begin the content analysis, still other variables will suggest themselves. Once you have completed your analysis, consider how you might use what you found with other members of your family. What kinds of patterns might you try to alter?

Activity 8.2: Telling a Story: Focusing on a Problem, Process, or Phenomenon

In this activity, you will be taking pictures for a specific purpose. The goal is not to take "good" pictures, if by good you mean them to be aesthetic or technically perfect. Aesthetics might be a plus, but not a necessity. Your assignment is to take pictures for purposes of assessment. Like any other assessment activity, you will be focusing on what is, what is likely to be, or what ought to be. First you will need to decide what it is that you want to uncover. Then you will have to design a "shooting script" or "scenario." You do not need fancy equipment. You do need a clear idea.

Pick a subject with which you are familiar. Examples include:

- traffic patterns downtown or at an intersection near your home
- children or child-parent interactions in a nearby park or playground
- the living arrangements of older people in a nursing home or adult foster home
- the people who stand around or pass a given landmark
- shopping at the neighborhood market

Add others to the inventory, and then pick your subject. What is it you want to find out? What are the best times to photograph? Should you take pictures at different times of the day or week? Should you be selective regarding what you shoot, or should you shoot at random (for example, taking one photo every fifteen minutes at a given intersection, or four photos every fifteen minutes—one in each direction)? How can you combine a content analysis technique with your shooting script?

Have fun. And be sure to bring along enough film.

USING PHOTOGRAPHY IN YOUR PRACTICE: WORKING WITH OR ON BEHALF OF CLIENTS AND COLLEAGUES

Now that you have had some practice on your own, it is time to consider using photography as a bona fide assessment tool in your practice. What kinds of ideas did Illustrations 8.1 and 8.2 suggest to you? Who might be helped by your use of photography? Do you have to take all the pictures, or can you work with available photographs? For example, in family therapy, could you use someone else's photographs in addition to a client's family album? What kind of responses might you get if you asked people to contrast their own family photos with others founds in one of the many excellent photobooks available in most full-line bookstores? Would you use a book of Diane Arbus photos, which tend to focus on the bizarre in human behavior? of Roy DeCarava's work, which concentrates on the essential aloneness of the individual, even in a crowd? Are there images in the *Family of Man* or *Family of Woman* you might want to explore with clients?

Whom might you involve in designing a shooting script? in taking the photographs? in interpreting their meaning? in hanging or displaying them? Where should they be displayed?

The sky is the limit. Anything between you and the sky is fair game. Go to it. And don't worry about perfect outcomes. You are now a pioneer in a new and relatively untried method that should have multiple applications to human service practice. Share your findings and your experiences with others.

SUGGESTIONS FOR FURTHER READING

Bill Aron, "A Disappearing Community," in Jon Wagner (ed.), *Images of Information.* Beverly Hills, CA: Sage Publications, 1979.

Howard S. Becker, "Do Photographs Tell the Truth?" *Afterimage*, 5 (February 1978): 9-13.

Paul Byers, "Still Photography in the Systematic Recording and Analysis of Behavioral Data." *Human Organization*, 23 (1964): 78-84.

Darrell Cheatwood and Thomas Linquest, *The Human Image: Sociology and Photography.* New Brunswick, NJ: Transaction, 1976.

John Collier, *Visual Anthropology: Photography as a Research Method.* New York: Holt, Rinehart & Winston, 1967.

Paul Ekman, W. Friesen, and Paul Ellsworth, *Emotion in the Human Face: Guidelines for Research and an Integration of Findings.* New York: Pergamon, 1972.

Paolo Friere, *Pedagogy of the Oppressed.* New York: Seabury, 1973.

Doug Harper, *The Homeless Man: An Ethnography of Work Trains and Booze.* Doctoral dissertation, University of Michigan, Ann Arbor, 1975. (Available from University Microfilms.)

Dorothea Lange and Paul S. Taylor, *An American Exodus.* New Haven, CT: Yale University Press, 1969.

Christopher Musello, *Homemade Photography: A Study of Visual Intervention and Communication in Every Day Life.* Master's thesis, University of Pennsylvania, Annenberg School of Communications, 1977.

Gunter Rambow et al., "Das Sinel Eben Alles Bilder der Straube" in *Die Fotoaktion als Sorialev Eingrilt, Eine Dokumentation.* Franfurt Am Main: Syndikat, 1979.

Jacob Riis, *How the Other Half Lives.* New York: Dove, 1971. (Originally published in 1890.)

Ervin Zube, "Pedestrians and Wind," in Jon Wagner (ed.), *Images of Information,* Beverly Hills, CA: Sage Publications, 1979: 59-68.

9. PUTTING IT ALL TOGETHER

The Contingency Approach to Assessment

Final chapters have a way of being repetitious or dull. If that turns out to be the case, I'll only take half the blame. We will be writing this chapter together. Our objective is to design a "contingency approach" to assessment, one in which the use of one assessment tool may spark the use of another, or in which several tools will have been selected in advance to assess various aspects of a situation or practice problem. To put yourself in the proper frame of mind, you might want to think of a particular situation that needs assessment or, better still, think of yourself as a trainer or consultant helping other people to make effective use of the assessment tools in this book. Start by looking at Table 9.1.

You can use Table 9.1 much the way in which you might use the "mileage between cities" chart on a road map. In this case, however, we are less concerned with distances than we are with the kinds of connections and interconnections that can be made. As we write this chapter together, we will start a particular tool in the left-hand column (like ecomapping) and then explore how it might be used together with one of the other tools listed in the row across the top. Notice that most of the boxes are numbered. Use these numbers for specifying the kinds of situations in which each tool can be used. You will understand how to progress when we get started.

For my part, I will be referring back to the case illustrations given at the beginning of each of the tools chapters. You will want to draw from your own experiences and insights. Enough said. Let's get into it.

TABLE 9.1 Combining Assessment Tools

		1 *Mapping*	2 *Task Analysis*	3 *Nominal Group Technique*	4 *Delphi*	5 *Force Field Analysis*	6 *Gaming*	7 *Photography*
A	Mapping		A2	A3	A4	A5	A6	A7
B	Task Analysis	B1		B3	B4	B5	B6	B7
C	Nominal Group Technique	C1	C2		C4	C5	C6	C7
D	Delphi	D1	D2	D3		D5	D6	D7
E	Force Field Analysis	E1	E2	E3	E4		E6	E7
F	Gaming	F1	F2	F3	F4	F5		F7
G	Photography	G1	G2	G3	G4	G5	G6	

ECOMAPPING AND OTHER TOOLS

Supposing you were an adoptions worker using ecomapping with a client family, as suggested in Chapter 2. What other tools could you use? Several come to my mind. A family considering adoption might find it helpful to spell out all the tasks that must be performed by family members to accommodate the new child (A2). NGT (A3) might be used in a subsequent session to identify the problems that individual family members perceive as needing attention. FFA might then be used to develop a plan for overcoming some of these problems (A5). It would draw on information already surfaced through ecomapping and NGT. You might also locate a game (A6) that could be used for helping each family member assess what is in it for him or her and what penalties might have to be paid for adopting a child. Is there a "family win" strategy? How might a family album look with a new child? What about the child's biofamily? Should the child have his or her own album that reflects his or her origins (A7)? We have begun to move from assessment to making decisions about intervention strategies.

Let's do the same with the second example. You will recall that it deals with the effort of a newly appointed agency director to assess the task environment about his organization. An identical map might be designed by a community organizer or social planner concerned with impacting on the way the agency interacts with elements in its environment. A funding agency might have similar concerns. Task analysis can also be used to specify the responsibilities of individual staff members within the agency for maintaining interagency linkages. Task analysis might also be used to spell out the functional interdependence of the various units involved. We now have two ideas for box A2.

You have already begun to think of how NGT might be used to spell out the range of desirable or undesirable interagency linkages or the problems to be addressed and goals to be achieved through them (A3). Delphi might well prove helpful in exploring the range of desirable and feasible interorganizational exchanges (A4). FFA can be used to identify those forces that restrain the organization from making any changes or that might be activated in favor of change. It can also be used to identify those key actors who can make a difference (A5). LINK, one of the games included in Chapter 7, might prove particularly useful in exploring the range of strategies that could lead to more effective linkages, or even for involving the relevant parties in the design of interagency exchanges (A6).

Now it's your turn. Take a problem or issue with which you are concerned. Starting with the mapping tool; consider which other

Ecomapping

1. Describe the situation or situations in which you will have used ecomapping.

2. Now, spell out the range of ways in which you might use each of the other six tools.

   A2   Task analysis

   A3   Nominal group technique

   A4   Delphi

   A5   Force field analysis

   A6   Gaming

   A7   Photography

3. Which of these would you use first? In what order might the others   follow?

tools might be used in tandem or in subsequent steps. Use the space that follows to record your ideas.

Consider some of the other tools in different orders. For example, if you were to think of how to use force field analysis prior to thinking about the nominal group technique or task analysis, you might come up with some different applications.

TASK ANALYSIS AND OTHER TOOLS

Chapter 3 begins with three practice illustrations. In the first example, an agency was considering using a task bank in order to "save" and "withdraw" human resources as needed in times of shrinking fiscal resources. In the second example, a foster-case staff team divided responsibilities in ways that were functional for the organization and that articulated with the strengths or interests of individual staff. In the third example, a community organizer used task analysis to specify the responsibilities of different agencies in establishing a case management system.

Take any one of those situations, or one in which you are currently involved, and think through how you might link one of the other six tools with task analysis. Which would you use first? With whom? How might they be linked to each other? In my own experience, I have found it productive to use Delphi as a means of designing a competency model as well as for projecting the difficulties in moving an agency's staff to perform new and untried or unfamiliar tasks. Force field analysis is exceptionally well suited for identifying the restraining and driving forces that lead to certain staff behaviors and levels of performance. Gaming might be useful in introducing staff members to the use of task analysis and to the notion of withdrawing from a bank of savings. Photography might serve as a tool for illustrating the process, for analysis of the kinds of tasks performed by workers, or for generating feedback on the complexity or difficulty of performing given tasks in specific environments. Ecomapping can help us in efforts to assess the psychological and social space between staff and around prescribed tasks.

Now it is your turn to spell out the connections.

Task Analysis

1. Describe the situation or situations in which you will have used task analysis.

2. Now, spell out the range of ways in which you might use each of the other six tools.

   B1   Ecomapping

   B3   Nominal group technique

   B4   Delphi

   B5   Force field analysis

   B6   Gaming

   B7   Photography

3. Which of these would you use first? In what order might the others follow?

NOMINAL GROUP TECHNIQUE
AND OTHER TOOLS

In the first illustration for Chapter 4, a worker describes how
NGT was used to enable members of a widow-to-widow group to
begin the self-help process. In the second example, a community
worker uses NGT to set priorities at the neighborhood level. How
could photography have been used in tandem with NGT, before
using NGT, and after using it? Could you build a nominal group
activity into an interactive gaming activity? Think about the
bridge-building game in Chapter 7. Could NGT be used in the
process of setting evaluative criteria for bridge design? Could
NGT be built into the LINK game to specify community or
interagency priorities? To what extent might NGT follow a force
field analysis of a treatment group or neighborhood problem?
Could the widow-to-widow group use FFA as a means of
understanding some of the difficulties all newly widowed persons
face, and how those difficulties might be overcome? To what
extent might ecomapping be useful in helping members of a self-
help group or neighborhood association understand where they
are in relationship to their environments and in relation to the
problems or priorities they have identified through NGT? Can
they use task analysis as a means of changing their relationships
to elements in their role sets or task environments? You will recall
that I built task analysis into the Team Planning Technique
described in Activity 4.2.

It is your turn again.

Nominal Group Technique

1. Describe the situation or situations in which you will have used nominal group technique.

---

2. Now, spell out the range of ways in which you might use each of the other six tools.

    C1   Ecomapping

    C2   Task analysis

    C4   Delphi

    C5   Force field analysis

    C6   Gaming

    C7   Photography

---

3. Which of these would you use first? In what order might the others   follow?

DELPHI AND OTHER TOOLS

Got the hang of it? Let's try the same approach to contingency planning with Delphi. I included only three illustrations in Chapter 5, but I am certain you can think of a variety of other situations in which Delphi might be used in policy analysis, agency/program design and in-service training, community planning, and so on. Consider designing a game that incorporates the policy or program recommendations that flow out of a series of Delphi iterations. You might find it a useful way to explore the implications of those recommendations and to test the accuracy of respondent perceptions of feasibility.

The game might include elements of force field analysis. Alternatively, FFA might be included in one of the Delphi iterations as a way of probing for the differences in respondent perception of feasibility. At the other end of the Delphi process, you might consider including a mapping exercise in the first iteration as a way of involving respondents in specifying the significant aspects of the task environment that must be acted on in order to achieve a given policy or program objective. You could also use it in determining what those objectives should be. A task analysis might flow from recommendations made by a respondent panel. Could photographs be used in the Delphi process? In one assessment study in which I participated, residents were asked to respond to photo images of different kinds of houses and neighborhood conditions in terms of acceptability, target for change, and the like.

Now it is your turn again. Think through a situation in which you might use the Delphi process and identify the other tools that might supplement it or be used in tandem.

Delphi

1. Describe the situation or situations in which you will have used the Delphi process.

2. Now, spell out the range of ways in which you might use each of the other six tools.

   D1   Ecomapping

   D2   Task analysis

   D3   Nominal group technique

   D5   Force field analysis

   D6   Gaming

   D7   Photography

3. Which of these would you use first? In what order might the others follow?

FORCE FIELD ANALYSIS
AND OTHER TOOLS

By now we have already considered the integration of FFA with four other tools. Other applications are possible. Remember the "Empire Strikes Back" in Chapter 6? If you were working with the same group of boys, how might you use photography for assessment or decision-making purposes? Could the boys develop a group home "family album" that includes images that might be amenable to change through use of FFA? Would gaming be helpful in reaching the boys how to be more assertive and responsible in the decision-making process or for changing the way they relate to adult authority? Could mapping techniques similar to those used in a treasure hunt be used for assessment purposes by the boys together with their worker? You have probably already identified some possible uses of the nominal group technique. How could you modify the Delphi process for kids of this age group?

GAMING AND OTHER TOOLS

We have seen how other tools might be incorporated directly into the design and play of a game. If you examine the descriptions of games in the most recent edition of the *Guide to Simulation/Games* referred to in Chapter 7, you will find other examples. LINK and its forerunner, COMPACTS, have often been used together with other assessment tools. Take a game with which you are familiar and consider the range of possibilities. If you have not had much experience with the use or design of gamed simulations, put yourself into the role of an urban planner who wishes to make professional use of a game like "Monopoly."

Assuming some modification in the design itelf so that it more adequately reflects current land use and investment realities, how might you use the following tools: Delphi, photography, NGT, task analysis, mapping, force field analysis? Would you build these directly into the game or use some prior to playing or as part of the redesign process? Might others flow from the experience of playing the game? How would these tools assist in the assessment, decision-making, or program and intervention design process?

Force Field Analysis

1. Describe the situation or situations in which you will have used the Delphi process.

---

2. Now, spell out the range of ways in which you might use each of the other six tools.

    E1   Ecomapping

    E2   Task analysis

    E3   Nominal group technique

    E4   Delphi

    E6   Gaming

    E7   Photography

---

3. Which of these would you use first? In what order might the others follow?

Use the form that follows to answer these questions in reference to "Monopoly" or another simulation/game with which you are familiar.

PHOTOGRAPHY

Let's take a trip into one of the neighborhoods up for grabs in "Monopoly," and let's bring our cameras. Suppose we were to use photographs in much the same way as described by the community organizer in the second vignette in Chapter 8. At what point might you use the photo images themselves in the conduct of a nominal group process aimed at prioritized community goals or action strategies? As we have seen, photos can be used to stimulate panel responses on a Delphi questionnaire. How might they be used to stimulate the examination of restraining and driving forces in an FFA? To what extent can they be built into or serve as an addendum to an ecomapping process? Could task statements be made more clear through the use of photo images? Could photo images be used to heighten awareness such that an otherwise resistant agency staff might agree to participate in a task analysis process? How?

Starting with a photo-image project in which you are interested, explore the range of linkages with other tools.

THE CONTINGENCY APPROACH

There is not much more to suggest. The rest is in your hands. Clearly, assessment is a creative activity. One needs an idea of what to look at as well as creativity in how one looks. Whatever tool you use—ecomapping, task analysis, nominal group, Delphi, force field analysis, gaming, or photography—you are likely to see something different. Each tool helps you to focus on some aspect of reality, alone or together with others. But like a good photographer, you are the one who must decide what it is you want to focus on.

Gaming

1. Describe the situation or situations in which you will have used gaming.

2. Now, spell out the range of ways in which you might use each of the other six tools.

    F1   Ecomapping

    F2   Task analysis

    F3   Nominal group technique

    F4   Delphi

    F5   Force field analysis

    F7   Photography

3. Which of these would you use first? In what order might the others follow?

Photography

1. Describe the situation or situations in whch you will have used photography.

2. Now, spell out the range of ways in which you might use each of the other six tools.

   G1   Ecomapping

   G2   Task analysis

   G3   Nominal group technique

   G4   Delphi

   G5   Force field analysis

   G6   Gaming

3. Which of these would you use first? In what order might the others follow?

You can focus on the here-and-now, on what is to be, or on what you think ought to be. But your choices are even broader than that. You can focus on a client or consumer population and its needs to overcome debilitating attitudes, lack of knowledge, or inadequate skill. Alternatively, you can focus on the availability, accessibility, effectiveness, efficiency, or responsiveness of a service program. Finally, you might choose to focus on comprehensiveness or the continuity of services.

You have taken the biggest step already by exploring the range of approaches possible and by trying a number of the assessment tools described in this book. You may already have already had some experience with one or more of these tools when you began to read the book. Practice will enable you to increase your expertise with each of the other tools. More important, it will provide you with a set of skills to do what you entered the human services for—to be of service in a professional manner.

ABOUT THE AUTHOR

ARMAND LAUFFER, editor of this series, is Professor of Social Work at the University of Michigan where he chairs the Community Organization Program and where he has been director of the University's Continuing Education Program in the Human Services, the largest, most varied program of its kind in the country. He frequently serves as a visiting professor at the Hebrew University of Jerusalem, and consults regularly with Israeli social agencies. Professor Lauffer has written or edited nearly 20 books in English and Hebrew, many of them dealing with resource development and social planning.

9492